Dutch Oven Bread Cookbook

120 Easy-to-Follow Homemade Bread Recipes Tailored for Beginners and Expert Bakers

Carlena B. Reese

ISBN-13: 979-8880340712

DEDICATION

To every one of my readers!

TABLE OF CONTENT

Introduction

Let's dive into the wonderful world of Dutch oven bread, where simplicity meets deliciousness. Dutch oven bread has been winning over hearts and taste buds with its rustic charm and mouthwatering flavors. This baking method brings together the best of both worlds: a crispy crust that crackles under your knife and a soft, pillowy interior that practically melts in your mouth. It's a bread that speaks of tradition and comfort, inviting you to slow down and savor each bite.

What sets Dutch oven bread apart is its unique baking process. By harnessing the heat-trapping qualities of a heavy pot, we create the perfect environment for bread to rise and develop its signature texture. The Dutch oven acts like a mini oven within your oven, allowing for even heat distribution and that coveted crust formation. It's a technique that has been passed down through generations, and for good reason—the results are simply divine.

One of the most delightful aspects of Dutch oven bread is its versatility. Whether you're craving a hearty sourdough, a fragrant rosemary loaf, or a simple white bread, the Dutch oven can handle it all. With a few basic ingredients and a bit of patience, you can create bakery-worthy bread right in your own kitchen. Plus, there's something incredibly satisfying about pulling a freshly baked loaf from the oven and filling your home with its irresistible aroma.

But Dutch oven bread isn't just about the end result; it's about the journey. There's a certain magic in the process of mixing flour, water, yeast, and salt and watching them transform into a golden-brown masterpiece. It's a hands-on experience that connects us to our food in a profound way, reminding us of the simple pleasures of homemade goodness.

Beyond its culinary appeal, Dutch oven bread also offers a sense of accomplishment. There's nothing quite like slicing into a loaf of bread that you've made from scratch, knowing that you've poured your heart and soul into every knead and fold. It's a reminder that good food doesn't have to be complicated—sometimes the most delicious things in life are the simplest.

In the pages ahead, we'll explore the ins and outs of Dutch oven bread, from selecting the perfect pot to mastering the art of shaping and scoring. Along the way, we'll share tips, tricks, and recipes to inspire your own bread-baking adventures. So roll up your sleeves, dust off your apron, and get ready to embark on a journey that's as rewarding as it is delicious. With Dutch oven bread, the possibilities are endless, and the results are always worth savoring.

Chapter 1: A Wonderful Way to Bake

Dutch oven bread has won the affection of bread lovers everywhere, giving you the freedom to create bread with a unique texture and flavor. Baking bread in a Dutch oven gives you that perfect combo of a crunchy crust on the outside and a soft, moist inside—something that's a bit tricky with regular baking methods. Let's dive into the magic of Dutch oven bread, uncover its advantages, and I'll toss in some tips and tricks to get you started on your own baking adventure.

What is Dutch Oven Bread?

Dutch oven bread is simply bread that's baked in a Dutch oven, which is a heavy-duty cooking pot with a snug lid, usually crafted from cast iron or enamel-coated cast iron. The Dutch oven's design ensures that heat is evenly spread and held, making it an ideal vessel for baking bread. This technique has become well-liked because of the outstanding bread it produces.

Picking the Perfect Dutch Oven for Bread Baking

When choosing a Dutch oven for baking bread, there are a couple of things to keep in mind. Firstly, make sure it's big enough to fit the size of the loaf you're planning to bake. A 5- to 6-quart Dutch oven usually works well for most bread recipes. As for material, go for either cast iron or enameled cast iron—they're both great at holding onto heat. Also, look for a Dutch oven with a lid that fits snugly, strong handles, and a smooth inside that's easy to clean up afterward.

Tips to Enhance Your Dutch Oven Bread

For that perfect Dutch oven bread, here are a few extra tricks to keep in mind:

- Make sure your Dutch oven's lid is heated up before baking to get a nice steam boost in the beginning.
- Get creative with slashing the dough before it hits the oven; it adds a lovely touch to the crust.
- If you fancy a more rustic flavor, mix in different flours, like rye or whole wheat.
- Toss in some extras like olives, cheese, or herbs to give your bread an extra flavor kick.
- Patience is key; let your bread cool wholly before you slice it to avoid any gummy situations.

With these tips, you'll take your Dutch oven bread to a whole new level of deliciousness and texture.

Common Mistakes You Should Avoid

While making bread in a Dutch oven is pretty straightforward, there are a few typical slip-ups to steer clear of:

- Don't let the dough ovenproof; it can make your loaf collapse or turn dense. Stick to the suggested rising times.
- Make sure to preheat the Dutch oven; this ensures a nice, crispy crust. Pop it in the oven with the heat on.
- Don't play fast and loose with the flour; using too little or too much can mess with your bread's texture. Stick to the recipe measurements.
- Patience is a virtue; resist the urge to remove the lid too soon. Let that bread rise at its own pace.
- Hold off on slicing into your masterpiece while it's still hot; you'll

end up with a gummy situation. Let it cool down before you dive in.

By keeping these slip-ups in check, you'll be well on your way to perfect Dutch oven bread.

Caring for Your Dutch Oven

To keep your Dutch oven in top shape and ensure it delivers perfect bakes every time, it's important to give it some tender, loving care. Here are a few pointers:

- Keep your cast iron Dutch oven seasoned regularly to prevent rust and enhance its non-stick surface.
- When it's cleaning time, steer clear of steel wool or harsh detergents. Stick to using a soft brush and hot water instead.
- Your Dutch oven should be stored in a dry spot to avoid the buildup of moisture.

- Mind the weight of your Dutch oven; it can be hefty. Use those tough handles or call for a helping hand when moving it around.

With these care tips, your Dutch oven will be your trusty sidekick in all your bread-baking escapades.

Storing Your Dutch Ovens Right

When it comes to keeping your Dutch ovens in tip-top shape, here are some handy tips:

- Before tucking them away, make sure your Dutch ovens are sparkling clean and fully dry.
- Opt for an easy-to-reach spot, preferably at chest height. These pots can get pretty heavy, so having them within reach makes life easier. You can place yours permanently on the stove for convenience.

- If you're stacking them up, throw a felt or silicone mat between the pots and lids. It'll keep those rims in top-notch condition and prevent any unwanted dings.

Chapter 2: The Dutch Oven Advantage

In the world of bread baking, there's no shortage of methods and gadgets to help you nail that ideal loaf. One tool that's become a favorite among home bakers is the Dutch oven. But why all the fuss about using a Dutch oven for baking bread?

Let's dig deeper into the world of baking bread with a Dutch oven and discover how it can take your homemade bread game up a notch.

The Power of Steam

What makes a Dutch oven a rock star in bread baking is its talent for whipping up a steamy atmosphere inside.

Steam plays a vital role in bread-making, lending that perfect combo of a crispy, golden crust and giving the bread enough room to swell up nicely in the oven.

Thanks to the snug lid on the Dutch oven, it captures the steam released by the dough, giving you a taste of the kind of steam action you find in fancy bakery ovens.

Heat Preservation and Consistent Baking

Dutch ovens, often crafted from cast iron, excel at retaining heat and spreading it evenly.

By preheating the Dutch oven and popping your bread in, you're creating a steady and strong heat that envelops the dough, giving you a perfectly risen and uniformly baked loaf.

Step-by-Step Guide to Baking Bread in a Dutch Oven

Here's a straightforward guide on how to bake bread in a Dutch oven:

Selecting the Perfect Dutch Oven

Before diving into baking bread with your Dutch oven, make sure it's oven-friendly and doesn't have any parts that could melt or catch fire.

- Opt for a standard oval or round Dutch oven with a lid for the best bread-baking experience.
- An enameled cast iron Dutch oven is a dependable and versatile kitchen tool.
- Look for a Dutch oven crafted from top-notch cast iron that distributes heat evenly and holds it well.
- Choose one with a tough enamel coating, available in various colors to match your kitchen style.
- Make sure it's got sturdy loop handles, a stainless steel knob, and a snug lid for durability and easy use.

Invest in an oven-safe Dutch oven that can handle temperatures up to 500°F (260°C), perfect for simmering, braising, roasting, and, of course, baking your favorite loaves of bread.

Getting the Dutch Oven Ready

Before you dive into baking your bread recipe in the Dutch oven, preheating is key.

- Simply pop your Dutch oven with no content into the oven and crank up the heat to your preferred temperature for baking (commonly around 230°C or 450°F). Let it warm up for 30 minutes or more.
- This step sees to it that both the lid and the pot are piping hot and ready to go for your bread.

Preparing and Shaping the Dough

While the Dutch oven is heating up, it's time to shape the bread dough just the way you like it.

Feel free to get inventive with various bread shapes, whether they're baguettes or boules.

Make sure your dough has had enough time to proof before you pop it into the hot Dutch oven.

Steam Baking

- Once the dough is all set and the Dutch oven is sizzling, carefully take the pot out of the oven.
- Sprinkle a bit of cornmeal or flour on the bottom to stop it from sticking, then carefully transfer the prepared dough into the pot.
- Give the dough's top a few slashes to let it expand while it bakes, place the hot lid over the Dutch oven to cover it, and slide it back into the oven.
- The Dutch oven will capture the steam given off by the dough as it is baking, creating the best setting for a crispy, deliciously browned crust.
- Take off the lid after approximately 20–30 minutes to let the bread bake fully and get that lovely crust that is golden-brown.

To sum it up, a Dutch oven is truly a fantastic tool for baking bread. Its knack for generating steam, along with its capacity to retain heat and ensure consistent baking, earns it high marks among home bakers.

By sticking to a few straightforward steps, you can indulge in bakery-quality bread with a crunchy crust and a tender, tasty center.

If you're keen on elevating your homemade bread game, giving a Dutch oven a whirl is a surefire way to go; you won't regret it.

Chapter 3: Basic Breads

1. Easy-Yeast Bread

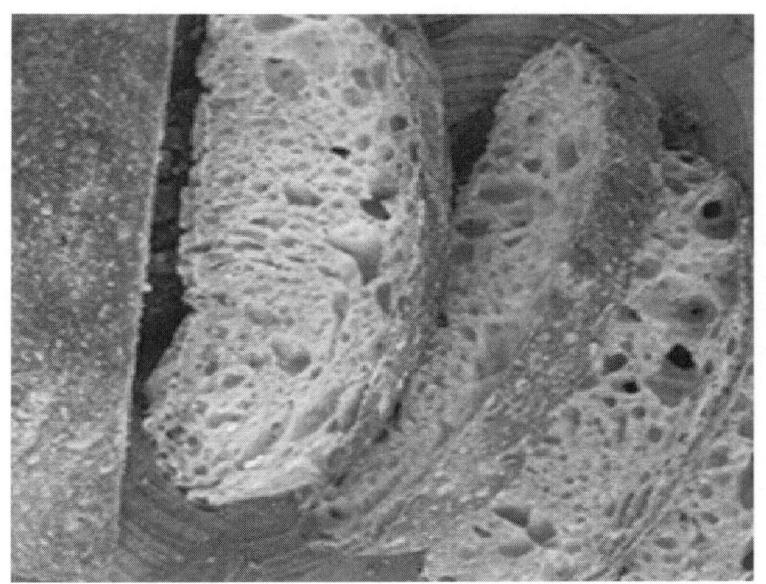

Prep Time: 10 minutes

Cook Time: 45 minutes

Serves: 10 servings

Ingredients

1 ½ cups water, warm

2 cloves of roasted garlic, minced

1 ½ teaspoons salt

2 teaspoons of active dry yeast

3 cups of white flour

Preparation

1. In a big bowl, add salt, garlic, yeast, and white flour.

2. Mix the flour mixture until combined.

3. Gradually add warm water to the flour mixture and mix until a dough is formed.

4. Use an olive oil cooking spray to spray a plastic wrap.

5. Use the sprayed plastic wrap to cover the dough bowl.

6. Also, use a wet kitchen towel to cover the dough bowl.

7. Set aside the dough for 18 to 24 hours at room temperature.

8. Heat up an oven to 450° Fahrenheit.

9. Place a Dutch oven with a lid in the oven.

10. On a floured work surface, transfer the dough and shape the dough into a round shape.

11. Cover the dough with a floured tea towel for 10 minutes.

12. Transfer the dough to a piece of parchment paper.

13. Gently transfer the dough to the heated Dutch oven and place a lid on the pot.

14. Return the Dutch oven to the oven.

15. Bake the dough for 30 minutes.

16. Remove the Dutch oven lid and bake the bread for 15 minutes more.

17. Transfer the bread to a cooling rack to cool and slice.

18. Serve the bread or transfer it to a well-lidded container and freeze for 2 months.

Nutritional Information/Serving

Calories: 121 kcal, Protein: 3.8g, Fiber: 1.2g, Carbohydrates: 26g

2. Tasty Wheat Bread

Prep Time: 10 minutes

Cook Time: 45 minutes

Serves: 10 servings

Ingredients

½ tsp. salt

3 cups flour, whole-wheat

1 tsp. agave nectar

1 tsp. active dry yeast

1 ½ cups of water (100° F)

Preparation

1. In a bowl, add water, agave nectar, and dry yeast, and mix together.

2. Set aside the yeast mixture for 15 minutes.

3. In another big bowl, add the whole wheat flour and salt, and mix together.

4. Pour the yeast mixture into the flour mixture, and mix until combined.

5. Knead the dough gently for a few minutes.

6. Use a plastic wrap to cover the dough and set aside for 10 hours at room temperature.

7. On a floured work surface, transfer the dough and, using floured hands, knead the dough until a smooth texture is formed.

8. Shape the dough into a round shape and set aside for a few minutes.

9. Heat an oven to 450° Fahrenheit.

10. Place a lidded Dutch oven in the oven for about 20 minutes.

11. Transfer the dough into the hot Dutch oven and cover with a lid.

12. Place the Dutch oven in the oven and bake the dough for 30 minutes.

13. Uncover the Dutch oven and bake the bread for 10–15 minutes, or until brown.

14. Transfer the wheat bread to a cooling rack to cool, slice, and serve.

Nutritional Information/Serving

Calories: 125 kcal, Protein: 5g, Carbohydrates: 27g, Fat: 1g

3. Easy White Bread

Prep Time: 10 minutes

Cook Time: 45 minutes

Serves: 8 servings

Ingredients

1 ½ cups warm water

½ teaspoon rapid-rise yeast

1 tsp. of salt

3 cups of white flour

Preparation

1. Add water, yeast, salt, and white flour to a mixing bowl.

2. Mix the flour mixture until a dough is formed.

3. Use a plastic wrap to cover the dough.

4. Set aside the dough for 2 hours.

5. Transfer the dough to a floured, plain surface.

6. Shape the dough into a round shape.

7. Return the dough to the bowl, cover, and set aside for 30 minutes.

8. Place a Dutch oven with a lid in the oven and heat up the oven to 450° Fahrenheit.

9. Gently transfer the dough to the hot Dutch oven and cover with the lid.

10. Bake the dough for 30 minutes.

11. Uncover the Dutch oven and bake the bread for 10 to 15 minutes more.

Nutritional Information/Serving

Calories: 172 kcal, Protein: 5g, Fiber: 1g, Carbohydrates: 36g, Fat: 1g

4. Healthy Soda Bread

Prep Time: 10 minutes

Cook Time: 30 minutes

Serves: 4 servings

Ingredients

1 cup of buttermilk

1/2 tsp. salt

1/2 tsp. baking soda

2 cups of white flour

Preparation

1. Place a Dutch oven with a lid in the oven.

2. Heat up the oven to 425° Fahrenheit.

3. In a bowl, add the buttermilk, salt, soda, and white flour.

4. Mix the flour mixture until a dough is formed.

5. On a work surface, transfer the dough and knead until a smooth texture is formed.

6. Shape the dough into a round shape.

7. Transfer the kneaded dough to the heated Dutch oven.

8. Use bread lame to score the top of the dough.

9. Bake the dough until golden, or for 20–30 minutes.

Nutritional Information/Serving

Calories: 265 kcal, Protein: 8g, Fiber: 2g, Carbohydrates: 51g, Fat: 3g

5. French Rustic Bread

Prep Time: 10 minutes

Cook Time: 50 minutes

Serves: 8 servings

Ingredients

1 ¼ cups warm water (105 degrees)

1 ½ tsp. dry yeast

1 teaspoon of salt

1 tsp. sugar

3 ¼ cups white flour (plus more for sprinkling)

Preparation

1. In a mixing bowl, add sugar, water, and dry yeast, and mix until combined.

2. Set aside the yeast mixture for 5 minutes.

3. Add salt and 2 cups of white flour to the yeast bowl and mix until combined.

4. Add 1 1/4 cups of white flour to the flour mixture and mix until a sticky dough is formed.

5. Lightly sprinkle flour in a bowl and on a piece of parchment paper.

6. Transfer the sticky dough to the floured bowl and use a clean tea towel to cover the dough.

7. Set aside the dough bowl for 2 hours.

8. Shape the dough into a smooth, round shape and transfer it to the floured parchment paper.

9. Lightly sprinkle flour over the dough.

10. Use a big bowl to cover the dough for 30 minutes.

11. In an oven, place a Dutch oven that has a lid and heat up the oven for 20 minutes.

12. Transfer the shaped dough to the parchment paper.

13. Use a bread lame to score the dough top.

14. Transfer the scored dough to the heated Dutch oven.

15. Place a lid on the Dutch oven, and bake for 30 minutes at 425° Fahrenheit.

16. Uncover the Dutch oven and bake the bread until brown, or for 20 minutes more.

17. Gently transfer the French rustic bread to a wire rack to cool and slice.

18. Serve the French rustic bread or transfer to a well-lidded container and store for 3 to 5 days.

Nutritional Information/Serving

Calories: 130 kcal, Protein: 3.8g, Fiber: 1.2g, Carbohydrates: 26.5g, Fat: 0.6g

6. Simple Oatmeal Bread

Prep Time: 10 minutes

Cook Time: 45 minutes

Serves: 8 servings

Ingredients

½ tsp. salt

1 tsp. dry active yeast

325 ml of warm water

100 g of old-fashioned oats

400 g bread flour

Preparation

1. Add water, oats, and flour to a mixing bowl.

2. Mix the flour mixture until combined.

3. Knead the dough for 5 minutes and cover the dough with plastic wrap.

4. Set aside the dough for 60 minutes.

5. Sprinkle yeast and salt on the dough.

6. Knead the dough for 15 minutes and cover the dough again.

7. Set aside the dough for 90 minutes.

8. Flatten the dough lightly and shape the dough into a round shape.

9. Place a sheet of parchment paper in a Dutch oven and transfer the shaped dough to the pot.

10. Cover the Dutch oven with a lid and set it aside at a warm temperature for 30 minutes.

11. Use a bread lame to score the dough top.

12. Cover the Dutch oven with a lid and transfer to an oven.

13. Bake the dough for 40–45 minutes at 450 degrees Fahrenheit.

14. Transfer the oatmeal bread to a cooling rack to cool, slice, and serve.

Nutritional Information/Serving

Calories: 228 kcal, Protein: 7.6g, Fiber: 2.5g, Carbohydrates: 44.7g, Fat: 1.6g

7. No Knead Yeast and Wheat Bread

Prep Time: 5 minutes

Cook Time: 50 minutes

Serves: 12 servings

Ingredients

3 ¾ cups flour, whole wheat

1 tsp. dry active yeast

2 tsp. salt

2 cups warm water (110 Fahrenheit)

Preparation

1. Add salt, yeast, and whole wheat flour to a big bowl and mix together.

2. Gently add the warm water to the flour mixture and mix until a dough is formed.

3. Use a tea towel to cover the dough bowl and set aside for 8 hours at room temperature.

4. Lightly sprinkle flour on a work surface.

5. Transfer the dough to the floured work surface.

6. Shape the dough into a round shape with floured hands and set aside.

7. Place a Dutch oven with a lid in the oven and heat up the oven to 450° Fahrenheit.

8. Gently transfer the dough to the heated Dutch oven and cover with the lid.

9. Bake the dough for 30 minutes.

10. Uncover the Dutch oven and bake the bread for 20 minutes more.

11. Transfer the yeast and wheat bread to a cooling rack to cool and slice.

12. Serve the bread or transfer it to a well-lidded container and freeze for 3 days.

Nutritional Information/Serving

Calories: 130 kcal, Protein: 5g, Fiber: 4g, Carbohydrates: 27g, Fat: 1g

8. No Knead Raisin and Cinnamon Bread

Prep Time: 10 minutes

Cook Time: 45 minutes

Serves: 8 servings

Ingredients

2 tablespoons of maple syrup

1/3 cup of brown sugar

1 1/2 cups warm water (105 Fahrenheit)

1 cup of raisins

1 tablespoon cinnamon

1 teaspoon salt

1/2 teaspoon active dry yeast

3 cups of white flour

Preparation

1. Add raisins, cinnamon, salt, yeast, and white flour to a big mixing bowl.

2. Mix the flour mixture until combined.

3. Add water to the flour mixture and mix until a sticky dough is formed.

4. Use a plastic wrap to cover the dough and set aside for 3 to 5 hours.

5. Place a lidded Dutch oven in the oven.

6. Heat up the oven for 30 to 40 minutes at 450 degrees Fahrenheit.

7. Transfer the sticky dough to a floured work surface.

8. Use floured hands to gently fold the dough over itself once.

9. Add the remaining ingredients to the dough.

10. Fold the dough gently over itself three times.

11. Shape the dough into a tight round shape.

12. In a bowl, lay a sheet of parchment paper and add the dough to the lined bowl.

13. Use a tea towel to cover the dough for 20 minutes.

14. Gently transfer the dough, with the paper, to the heated Dutch oven.

15. Score the top of the dough with a bread lame.

16. Cover the Dutch oven with a lid and bake the dough for 30 minutes.

17. Remove the lid of the Dutch oven and bake the dough for 15 minutes more.

18. Transfer the bread to a cooling rack to cool, slice, and serve.

Nutritional Information/Serving

Calories: 281 kcal, Protein: 5.6g, Fiber: 2.7g, Carbohydrates: 64.4g, Fat: 0.5g

9. Yummy Monkey Bread

Prep Time: 5 minutes

Cook Time: 25 minutes

Serves: 6 servings

Ingredients

Powdered sugar glaze (to drizzle)

1 (16-ounce) tube of refrigerated biscuits

1/2 cup of walnuts, chopped

2 tbsp. cinnamon

1/4 cup brown sugar

1/4 cup white sugar

4 tbsp. butter, melted

Preparation

1. Place a lidded Dutch oven in the oven.

2. Heat up the oven to 350° Fahrenheit.

3. In a plastic bag, add the chopped walnuts, cinnamon, and sugars, and mix together.

4. Break the biscuit into pieces.

5. Add the biscuits to the walnut mixture and toss until evenly coated.

6. Add the melted butter to the heated Dutch oven.

7. Add the coated biscuits to the heated Dutch oven and mix until evenly coated.

8. In a single layer, spread the coated biscuits in the Dutch oven.

9. Place a lid on the Dutch oven and bake for 15 to 25 minutes at 350° Fahrenheit.

10. Transfer the bread to a cooling rack to cool.

11. Garnish with the glaze and serve.

Nutritional Information/Serving

Calories: 205 kcal, Protein: 2g, Fiber: 2g, Carbohydrates: 21g, Fat: 14g

10. Honeyed, No Knead Bread

Prep Time: 10 minutes

Cook Time: 50 minutes

Serves: 10 servings

Ingredients

2 cups water, warm

2 tbsp. honey

1 tsp. active dry yeast

1 tsp. salt

1 cup of oats

3 ¾ cups white flour

Preparation

1. Add yeast, salt, oats, and white flour to a big bowl and mix until combined.

2. Add the honey and water to the flour mixture and mix until a dough is formed.

3. Use plastic wrap to cover the dough bowl and set aside for 12–24 hours.

4. Place a Dutch oven with a lid in the oven and heat up the oven to 450 degrees Fahrenheit.

5. Lightly sprinkle flour on the dough.

6. Shape the dough into a round shape with floured hands.

7. Transfer the shaped dough to a sheet of parchment paper.

8. Use a bread lame to score the top of the dough.

9. Transfer the scored dough to the heated Dutch oven with the parchment paper.

10. Place a lid on the Dutch oven and bake the dough for 30 minutes.

11. Uncover the Dutch oven and bake the bread until brown, or for 15-20 minutes.

12. Transfer the bread to a cooling rack to cool, slice, and serve.

Nutritional Information/Serving

Calories: 215 kcal, Protein: 6g, Fiber: 2g, Carbohydrates: 45g, Fat: 0.2g

11. Rosemary Garlic Bread

Prep Time: 10 minutes

Cook Time: 40 minutes

Serves: 8 servings

Ingredients

3 diced garlic cloves

2 big rosemary sprigs, destemmed and diced

1 1/3 cups of warm water

2 1/2 teaspoons of quick yeast

2 teaspoons of salt

1 1/2 teaspoons sugar

3 cups of white flour

Preparation

1. Add garlic, rosemary sprigs, water, yeast, salt, sugar, and white flour to a mixing bowl.

2. Mix the flour mixture until a sticky dough is formed.

3. Use a kitchen towel to cover the dough.

4. Set aside the dough at a warm temperature for 1 hour.

5. Use flour to dust a sheet of parchment paper.

6. On the floured paper, transfer the dough and shape the dough into a round shape.

7. Use a tea towel to cover the dough and set aside for 20 minutes.

8. Place a lidded Dutch oven in the oven and heat up the oven to 450 degrees Fahrenheit.

9. Transfer the dough into the hot Dutch oven with the parchment paper.

10. Use a bread lame to score the dough.

11. Place a lid on the Dutch oven, and transfer the pot to the heated oven.

12. Bake the dough for 30 minutes.

13. Remove the Dutch oven lid and bake the bread until brown, or for 10 minutes more.

14. Transfer the rosemary garlic bread to a cooling rack to cool, slice, and serve.

Nutritional Information/Serving

Calories: 187 kcal, Protein: 6g, Fiber: 2g, Carbohydrates: 38g, Fat: 1g

12. No Knead Crusty Bread

Prep Time: 10 minutes

Cook Time: 40 minutes

Serves: 10 servings

Ingredients

2 cups of warm water (125 degrees Fahrenheit)

1 1/2 teaspoons salt

2 teaspoons instant yeast

4 cups of white flour

Preparation

1. In a big bowl, add the yeast, salt, and white flour, and mix until combined.

2. Create a well in the middle of the flour mixture.

3. Add warm water to the middle of the flour mixture and mix until combined.

4. Use plastic wrap to cover the dough and set aside for 2 hours.

5. Gently press down the dough and shape it into a round shape.

6. Transfer the shaped dough to a big sheet of parchment paper.

7. Use a tea towel to cover the dough and set aside for 60 minutes.

8. Heat up an oven to 450 degrees Fahrenheit.

9. Place a Dutch oven with a lid in the heated oven for 30 minutes.

10. Transfer the dough with the parchment paper into the hot Dutch oven.

11. Place a lid on the Dutch oven and bake the dough for 30 minutes.

12. Uncover the Dutch oven and bake the dough for 10 minutes more.

13. Transfer the crusty bread to a cooling rack to cool, slice, and serve.

Nutritional Information/Serving

Calories: 307 kcal, Protein: 9g, Fiber: 2g, Carbohydrates: 64g, Fat: 0g

13. Healthy Ciabatta Bread

Prep Time: 25 minutes

Cook Time: 1 hour, 5 minutes

Serves: 12 servings

Ingredients

For Poolish:

¼ tsp. instant yeast

200 ml of room-temperature water

1 ½ cups of bread flour

For Dough:

½ tsp. instant yeast

2 tsp. salt

1 cup of room-temperature water

2 ⅔ cups bread flour

Preparation

For Poolish:

1. In a medium bowl, add the yeast, water, and bread flour, and mix until combined.

2. Use a plastic wrap to cover the flour mixture.

3. Set aside the flour mixture at room temperature for 15-20 hours.

For Dough:

4. In a mixing bowl, add yeast, salt, water, flour, and the poolish.

5. Mix together until a sticky dough is formed.

6. Use a nonstick cooking spray to lightly spray a big bowl.

7. Transfer the dough to the sprayed bowl.

8. Use a plastic wrap to cover the dough and set aside at room temperature for 60 minutes.

9. Stretch and fold the dough; use a plastic wrap to cover the dough; and set aside for 45 minutes.

10. Stretch and fold the dough again, use a plastic wrap to cover the dough, and set aside for another 45 minutes.

11. Place two Dutch ovens with lids in an oven.

12. Preheat the oven to 450 degrees Fahrenheit for 30 minutes.

13. Sprinkle flour on a plain surface and use two bench scrapers.

14. Transfer the dough to the floured surface.

15. Sprinkle flour on the dough top and use the bench scrapers to shape the dough into a square shape.

16. Evenly divide the dough into two and shape each of the dough into a loaf shape.

17. Transfer each of the shaped doughs to a sheet of parchment paper.

18. Transfer the dough with the parchment paper into the heated Dutch oven.

19. Place the lid on each Dutch oven and bake the dough for 30 minutes.

20. Remove the lids of the Dutch ovens and bake the breads for 25 to 35 minutes, or until brown.

21. Transfer the breads to cooling racks to cool and slice.

22. Serve the bread or wrap it with double layers of foil and freeze for 12 weeks.

Nutritional Information/Serving

Calories: 197 kcal, Protein: 7g, Fiber: 1g, Carbohydrates: 39g, Fat: 1g

14. Easy Beer Bread

Prep Time: 10 minutes

Cook Time: 55 minutes

Serves: 12 servings

Ingredients

1 ½ tsp. salt

350 mL of beer

½ tbsp. instant yeast

3 ¼ cups white flour

Preparation

1. Add salt, beer, yeast, and white flour to a big mixing bowl.

2. Mix the flour mixture until a dough is formed.

3. Knead the dough until a smooth dough is formed, or for 5 minutes.

4. Use a plastic wrap to cover the dough bowl and set aside for 1–1 1/2 hours.

5. Place a sheet of parchment paper in a Dutch oven.

6. Lightly sprinkle flour on the parchment paper.

7. Shape the dough gently into a round shape.

8. Transfer the shaped dough into the middle of the lined Dutch oven.

9. Set aside the Dutch oven for 60 minutes.

10. Score the top of the dough with bread lame.

11. Place a lid on the hot Dutch oven.

12. Transfer the Dutch oven to an oven.

13. Bake the dough for 25 minutes at 400 degrees Fahrenheit.

14. Uncover the Dutch oven and bake the dough for 30 minutes more.

15. Transfer the beer bread to a wire rack to cool and serve.

Nutritional Information/Serving

Calories: 137 kcal, Protein: 4g, Fiber: 1g, Carbohydrates: 27g, Sodium: 293mg

15. Artisan Bread

Prep Time: 10 minutes

Cook Time: 47 minutes

Serves: 8 servings

Ingredients

1 ½ cups warm water (120 degrees Fahrenheit)

1 ¾ tsp. salt

2 ¼ tsp. instant yeast

3 ¾ cups bread flour

Preparation

1. Add salt, yeast, and flour to a big mixing bowl and mix until combined.

2. Add warm water to the flour mixture and mix until a sticky dough is formed.

3. Use plastic wrap to cover the dough and set aside for 2 hours at room temperature.

4. Place a big Dutch oven that has a lid in the oven.

5. Heat up an oven to 450 degrees Fahrenheit for 30 minutes.

6. Stretch and fold the dough, and gently pinch any seams together in the middle of the dough.

7. Lightly sprinkle flour on a work surface.

8. Transfer the dough to the floured work surface with the seam part facing down.

9. Gently shape the dough into a round shape.

10. Transfer the shaped dough to the middle of a sheet of parchment paper.

11. Sprinkle flour on the top of the dough.

12. Use plastic wrap to cover the dough for 10 minutes.

13. Score the dough top with bread lame.

14. Transfer the bread to the heated Dutch oven and place a lid on the Dutch oven.

15. Bake the dough for 30 minutes.

16. Uncover the Dutch oven and bake the bread for 15–17 minutes, or until brown.

17. Transfer the artisan bread to a cooling rack to cool, slice, and serve.

Nutritional Information/Serving

Calories: 222 kcal, Protein: 8g, Fiber: 2g, Carbohydrates: 44g, Fat: 1g

Chapter 4: Holiday Breads

16. Finnish Christmas Bread

Prep Time: 15 minutes

Cook Time: 45 minutes

Serves: 6 servings

Ingredients

For Rye Scald:

1 tbsp. fennel seeds

⅔ cup of rye flour

¾ cup of boiling water

For Dough:

1 tbsp. soft butter

3 tbsp. molasses

¼ cup of lukewarm water

1 tsp. aniseed

1 tsp. salt

2 tsp. instant yeast

1 ¾ cups bread flour

Preparation

For Rye Scald:

1. Add fennel seeds, rye flour, and water to a small bowl.

2. Mix the flour mixture together and cover the bowl.

3. Set aside the flour mixture for 3 to 4 hours.

For Dough:

4. Add butter, molasses, water, aniseed, salt, yeast, bread flour, and rye scald to a medium bowl.

5. Mix the bread flour mixture until a dough is formed.

6. Knead the dough until a smooth dough is formed, or for 20 minutes.

7. Use a tea towel to cover the dough and set aside for 30 minutes.

8. Shape the dough into a round shape.

9. Transfer the dough to a parchment-paper-lined Dutch oven.

10. Place a lid on the Dutch oven and set aside for 1 hour 30 minutes at room temperature.

11. Heat up an oven to 450 degrees Fahrenheit.

12. Sprinkle flour on top of the dough and use bread lame to score the dough.

13. Cover the Dutch oven with a lid, and bake the dough for 20 minutes.

14. Reduce the oven temperature to 400 degrees Fahrenheit.

15. Uncover the Dutch oven and bake the bread for 25 minutes.

16. Transfer the Finnish Christmas bread to a cooling rack to cool, slice, and serve.

17. Transfer leftovers to a well-lidded container and freeze for 8 weeks or store for 3 days at room temperature.

Nutritional Information/Serving

Calories: 173 kcal, Protein: 3.9g, Fiber: 4.8g, Carbohydrates: 32.9g, Fat: 3.8g

17. Pita Bread

Prep Time: 10 minutes

Cook Time: 2 minutes

Serves: 16 servings

Ingredients

1½ tsp. salt

4 cups of white flour

¼ cup olive oil (plus more for brushing)

1 packet of instant yeast

2 tbsp. sugar

1 ½ cups water, warm

Preparation

1. Add yeast, sugar, and water to a medium bowl and mix until combined.

2. Set aside the sugar mixture for 5 minutes.

3. Add the remaining ingredients to the sugar mixture and mix until a dough is formed.

4. Use a tea towel to cover the dough and set aside for 45 minutes.

5. Gently punch down the dough and evenly divide the dough into 16 round shapes.

6. Use tea towels to cover the dough and set aside for 15 minutes.

7. Place a Dutch oven on medium-low heat.

8. Roll out each of the dough balls to a 1" thickness.

9. Use olive oil to lightly brush the top of each dough ball.

10. Place the oiled part of each dough ball in the heated Dutch oven.

11. Saute the dough until lightly golden, or for 30–60 seconds.

12. Flip the bread and sauté the other side for 30–60 seconds.

13. Saute the remaining dough ball and serve.

Nutritional Information/Serving

Calories: 151 kcal, Protein: 3g, Fiber: 1g, Carbohydrates: 26g, Fat: 4g

18. Easy Panettone

Prep Time: 15 minutes

Cook Time: 45 minutes

Serves: 12 servings

Ingredients

For Panettone Starters:

¼ cup sourdough starter

¼ cup of cold water

½ cup flour

For dried fruit:

¼ cup rum

½ cup pineapple, dried and diced

½ cup cherries, dried and quartered

½ cup golden raisins

For Dough:

6 tbsp. soft butter

1 ¼ tsp. salt

2 ½ cups white flour (plus extra for sprinkling)

1 tbsp. orange zest, freshly grated

1 tbsp. lemon zest, freshly grated

1 ½ tsp. vanilla extract

2 tbsp. white sugar

⅓ cup white sugar

2 big eggs

1 packet of active dry yeast

¼ cup of warm water

For Egg Wash:

1 tbsp. water

1 big egg

Preparation

For Panettone Starters:

1. In a bowl, add all the ingredients and mix until combined.

2. Cover the starter bowl and set it aside for 8 hours at room temperature.

For dried fruit:

3. In another bowl, add the pineapple, cherries, and raisins and mix together.

4. Add rum to the raisin mixture and mix together.

5. Set aside the dried fruit mixture for 8 hours (toss the fruit mixture accordingly).

For Dough:

6. In a big mixing bowl, add the yeast and water and mix together.

7. Set aside the yeast mixture for 10 minutes.

8. Add the lemon zest, orange zest, vanilla extract, sugars, and eggs to the yeast mixture and mix until combined.

9. Add the salt, white flour, and panettone starter to the yeast mixture and mix until a dough is formed.

10. Knead the dough until a smooth texture is formed.

11. Add the soft butter to the dough and knead for 5 minutes.

12. Transfer the dough to a plain surface.

13. Use a bench scraper and wet fingers to fold the dough into a round shape.

14. Return the shaped dough to the big mixing bowl.

15. Cover the dough and set aside for 3 hours, or until the dough doubles in size.

16. Return the dough to the plain surface and reshape the dough into a round shape.

17. Transfer the shaped dough to a plastic bag and refrigerate for 8 hours.

18. Take the dough from the refrigerator and roll it out into a flat rectangle shape.

19. Sprinkle flour over the dough.

20. Roll out the dough to a thickness of 1/2".

21. Add the fruit mixture to the top of the rolled dough and spread it.

22. Roll the dough with the fruit mixture into a log shape.

23. Gently roll the ends of the log towards the middle and smooth the dough into a round shape.

24. Place a paper panettone mold in a Dutch oven.

25. Transfer the shaped dough to the panettone mold and place a lid on the Dutch oven.

26. Set aside the dough for 3 to 4 hours.

27. Heat up an oven to 450° Fahrenheit.

For Egg Wash:

28. In a small bowl, add water and egg, and mix until combined.

29. Use the egg wash to brush the top of the dough.

30. Bake the dough for 30 minutes.

31. Uncover the Dutch oven and bake the bread for 10 to 15 minutes more.

32. On both sides of the panettone mold, poke 2 skewers and turn the bread upside down until it is cool.

33. Remove the skewers, slice, and serve.

Nutritional Information/Serving

Calories: 290 kcal, Protein: 6g, Carbohydrates: 47g, Fat: 8g

19. No-knead Rosemary Bread

Prep Time: 10 minutes

Cook Time: 45 minutes

Serves: 8 servings

Ingredients

1/4 cup olive oil

1 1/4 cups water (at room temperature)

2 tablespoons rosemary, freshly chopped

1 1/2 teaspoons salt

1/2 teaspoon instant yeast

15 ounces of white flour

Preparation

1. Add the rosemary, salt, instant yeast, and white flour to a big bowl and mix until combined.

2. Add oil and water to the flour mixture and mix until a sticky dough is formed.

3. Use a plastic wrap to cover the dough bowl and set it aside for 10 to 12 hours at room temperature.

4. Lightly sprinkle flour on a plain surface.

5. Transfer the dough to the floured surface.

6. Lightly sprinkle flour on the dough.

7. For a few times, gently fold over the dough and shape into a round shape.

8. Use a cooking spray to spray a sheet of parchment paper.

9. Transfer the shaped dough to the sprayed parchment paper.

10. Use a tea towel to cover the dough and set aside for 60 minutes.

11. Place a big Dutch oven with a lid in the oven.

12. Heat up the oven to 500 degrees Fahrenheit.

13. Transfer the shaped dough to the heated Dutch oven and place a lid on the pot.

14. Return the Dutch oven to the oven and bake the dough for 30 minutes at 425 degrees Fahrenheit.

15. Uncover the Dutch oven and bake the bread for 15 minutes more.

16. Transfer the rosemary bread to a cooling rack to cool, slice, and serve.

Nutritional Information/Serving

Calories: 254 kcal, Protein: 5.6g, Fiber: 1.6g,
Carbohydrates: 40.8g, Fat: 7.3g

20. No-Knead Cinnamon Bread

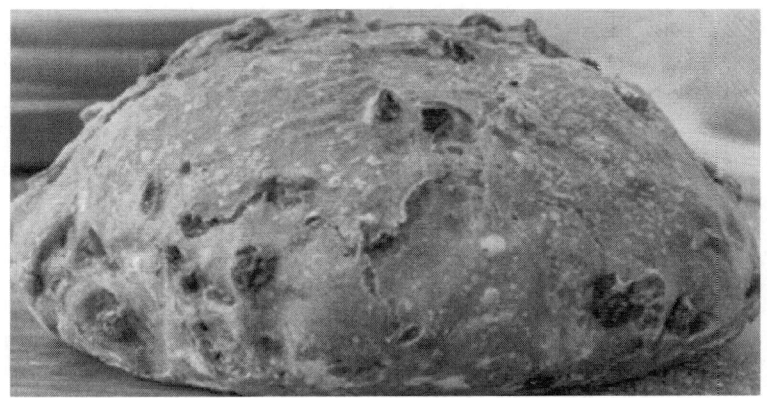

Prep Time: 10 minutes

Cook Time: 50 minutes

Serves: 10 servings

Ingredients

3 tbsp. brown sugar

1½ cups of lukewarm water (110 degrees Fahrenheit)

1 cup of raisins

1 tbsp. ground cinnamon

½ tsp. active dry yeast

1 tsp. salt

3 cups of white flour

Preparation

1. Add the raisins, cinnamon, yeast, salt, and white flour to a large bowl and mix until combined.

2. Add the lukewarm water to the flour mixture and mix until a dough is formed.

3. Use a plastic wrap to cover the dough bowl.

4. Set aside the dough for 12–18 hours at room temperature.

5. Place a Dutch oven with a lid in the oven.

6. Heat up the oven to 450 degrees Fahrenheit.

7. Sprinkle flour on a plain surface and transfer the dough to the floured surface.

8. Lightly sprinkle flour on the top of the dough.

9. Use a rolling pin to flatten the top of the dough.

10. Sprinkle the sugar over the top of the flattened part of the dough.

11. For a few times, fold the dough until the sugar lightly combines and fold into a round shape.

12. Transfer the shaped dough to a piece of parchment paper.

13. Transfer the dough with the paper to the heated Dutch oven.

14. Place a lid on the Dutch oven and bake the dough for 30 minutes.

15. Remove the lid of the Dutch oven and bake the bread until brown, or for 15-20 minutes.

16. Transfer the cinnamon bread to a cooling rack to cool.

17. Serve the bread or transfer to a well-lidded container and store for 4 days at room temperature or in a well-sealed freezer bag and freeze for 12 weeks.

Nutritional Information/Serving

Calories: 197 kcal, Protein: 5g, Fiber: 3g,
Carbohydrates: 44g, Fat: 1g

21. Tasty Naan Bread

Prep Time: 10 minutes

Cook Time: 4 minutes

Serves: 8 servings

Ingredients

Olive oil

¼ cup of Greek yogurt

1 egg

½ tsp. baking powder

2 tsp. salt

3 cups of white flour (plus more for
sprinkling)

2 tbsp. honey

2 ¼ tsp. active dry yeast

1 cup water, warm

Preparation

1. Add the water and yeast to a small bowl and mix until combined.

2. Add honey to the yeast mixture and mix until combined.

3. Cover the honey mixture and let it sit for a few minutes.

4. Add the baking powder, salt, and white flour to a big bowl and mix until combined.

5. Create a well in the middle of the flour mixture.

6. In another bowl, add the yogurt, egg, and yeast mixture and mix until combined.

7. Add the yeast mixture to the middle of the flour mixture.

8. On a floured, plain surface, transfer the dough and set aside for a few minutes.

9. Sprinkle flour on the dough and knead until a soft and smooth dough is formed.

10. Lightly spray a Dutch oven with a nonstick cooking spray.

11. Transfer the dough to the sprayed Dutch oven and cover with a lid.

12. Set aside the dough for 3 hours or until it has doubled in size.

13. On another lightly floured, plain surface, transfer the dough and evenly divide it into 8 pieces.

14. Shape each of the dough pieces into a round shape and roll them to 1/4" thickness.

15. On medium-high heat, place a Dutch oven over the heat.

16. Add a small amount of olive oil to the heated Dutch oven.

17. Add the dough to the hot oil (cook in batches).

18. Saute the dough until it begins to bubble, or for a couple of minutes.

19. Flip the dough and sauté the other side of the dough for a couple of minutes.

20. Serve the naan bread or transfer to a well-lidded container and store for 5 days or freeze for 3 months.

Nutritional Information/Serving

Calories: 210.33 kcal, Protein: 7.18g, Fiber: 2.19g, Carbohydrates: 42g, Fat: 1.49g

22. Eggnog-Nutmeg Bread

Prep Time: 10 minutes

Cook Time: 50 minutes

Serves: 8 servings

Ingredients

1 ½ cups of eggnog

¼ tsp. cinnamon

¼ tsp. nutmeg

½ tsp. salt

2 tsp. baking powder

2 ¼ cups of white flour

⅓ cup sour cream

2 tbsp. spiced rum

1 tsp. vanilla extract

2 eggs

½ cup soft butter

1 cup sugar, granulated

Preparation

1. Heat up an oven to 350° Fahrenheit.

2. Use a nonstick cooking spray to spray a Dutch oven.

3. In a mixing bowl, add the sugar and soft butter, and mix until fluffy, or for 1 to 2 minutes.

4. Add the sour cream, spiced rum, vanilla extract, and eggnog to the sugar mixture and mix until combined.

5. Add the nutmeg, cinnamon, salt, baking powder, and white flour to a medium bowl and mix until combined.

6. Add half of the sugar mixture to the flour mixture and mix until combined.

7. Add the remaining sugar mixture to the flour mixture and mix until a dough is formed.

8. Place the dough in the sprayed Dutch oven.

9. Place a lid over the Dutch oven.

10. Transfer the Dutch oven to the preheated oven.

11. Bake the dough for 30 to 35 minutes.

12. Uncover the Dutch oven and bake the bread for 10 to 15 minutes more, or until brown.

13. Transfer the eggnog nutmeg bread to a cooling rack to cool, slice, and serve.

Nutritional Information/Serving

Calories: 302 kcal, Protein: 6.8g, Sodium: 139.1mg, Carbohydrates: 48.5g, Fat: 8.6g

23. Cornmeal and Milk Bread

Prep Time: 5 minutes

Cook Time: 20 minutes

Serves: 6 servings

Ingredients

2 tbsp. melted butter (to grease the Dutch oven)

¼ cup cheddar cheese, shredded

1 (4 ounces) can of (drained) green chiles

1 tsp. salt

1 tbsp. baking powder

½ cup of white flour

1 cup of cornmeal

2 tbsp. honey

1 egg

1 cup of milk

Preparation

1. Add honey, egg, and milk to a bowl and mix until combined.

2. Add salt, baking powder, cornmeal, and white flour to the milk mixture and mix until combined.

3. Grease a Dutch oven with the butter.

4. Place the greased Dutch oven with the lid in the oven.

5. For 15 minutes, heat up the oven to 425 degrees Fahrenheit.

6. Transfer the dough to the heated Dutch oven.

7. Sprinkle the shredded cheese and green chiles over the top of the dough.

8. Place a lid on the Dutch oven.

9. Return the Dutch oven to the heated oven.

10. Bake the dough until brown or for 20 minutes.

Nutritional Information/Serving

Calories: 334 kcal, Protein: 14.4g, Fiber: 1g, Carbohydrates: 39.6g, Fat: 13.1g

24. Lemon and Coconut Bread

Prep Time: 15 minutes

Cook Time: 1 hour

Serves: 12 servings

Ingredients

For Filling:

1 tablespoon of lemon juice

1 teaspoon lemon zest

¼ cup cane sugar, organic

¼ cup liquid coconut butter

1/4 cup of white flour

For Icing:

Unsweetened coconut, shredded

⅛ teaspoon coconut extract

½ teaspoon lemon zest

1 tsp. of lemon juice

3 tablespoons sugar, powdered

¼ cup cream cheese, vegan

For Dough:

Vegan butter, unsalted

¼ teaspoon salt

1 teaspoon lemon zest

2 1/4 cups of white flour

1 ¼ teaspoons of active yeast

2 tablespoons cane sugar, organic

1 ¼ cups of warm coconut milk, full-fat

Preparation

For Filling:

1. In a bowl, add the lemon juice, zest, sugar, and coconut butter and mix until combined.

2. Set aside the sugar mixture for 60 minutes.

3. Add the white flour to the sugar mixture and stir until combined.

For Icing:

4. In another bowl, add all the icing ingredients except the shredded coconut and mix until combined.

For Dough:

5. In a big bowl, add the cane sugar and coconut milk, and mix until combined.

6. Add the active dry yeast to the coconut milk mixture and stir until combined.

7. Set aside the coconut milk mixture for 5 minutes.

8. Add the remaining ingredients to the coconut mixture and mix until a dough is formed.

9. Use a kitchen towel to cover the dough bowl.

10. Set aside the dough for 60 minutes at room temperature.

11. Sprinkle flour on a work surface.

12. Transfer the dough to the floured work surface and knead until a smooth dough is formed.

13. Gently roll out the dough into a 16 by 12" rectangle shape.

14. Add the fillings to the top of the dough and spread.

15. Shape the dough gently into a round shape and transfer it to a sheet of parchment paper.

16. Transfer the dough with the parchment paper to a Dutch oven.

17. Use a lid to cover the Dutch oven and transfer it to an oven.

18. Bake the dough for 30 minutes at 350 degrees Fahrenheit.

19. Uncover the Dutch oven and bake the bread for 30 minutes more, or until brown.

20. Transfer the lemon and coconut bread to a cooling rack to cool.

21. Top the bread with the icing and unsweetened coconut.

22. Serve the bread or transfer it to a well-lidded container and refrigerate for 3 days.

Nutritional Information/Serving

Calories: 530 kcal, Protein: 4.4g, Fiber: 3.1g, Carbohydrates: 87.4g, Fat: 19.7g

25. Saffron-Braided Bread

Prep Time: 15 minutes

Cook Time: 50 minutes

Serves: 8 servings

Ingredients

1 tablespoon of water

1 tablespoon of olive oil

3 1/2 cups of white flour (plus extra for sprinkling and kneading)

1 1/2 teaspoons salt

4 tablespoons of melted butter, unsalted

1 large egg yolk

3 big eggs

A pinch of saffron threads

1 1/2 teaspoons active dry yeast

1/4 cup sugar

1 cup water, lukewarm

Preparation

1. Add the saffron threads, dry yeast, sugar, and a cup of water to a bowl, and mix until combined.

2. Set aside the sugar mixture for 15 minutes.

3. Add the salt, butter, egg yolk, and 2 eggs to the sugar mixture and mix until combined.

4. Add the white flour to the sugar mixture and mix until a sticky dough is formed.

5. Sprinkle flour on a plain surface.

6. Transfer the dough to the floured, plain surface.

7. Knead the sticky dough for 10 minutes or until a smooth dough is formed (add flour to the dough if needed).

8. Use the olive oil to grease a medium bowl.

9. Transfer the dough to the greased bowl and turn the dough to coat it with the olive oil.

10. Use a tea towel to cover the dough and set aside for 60 minutes at a warm temperature.

11. Remove the towel from the dough, turn, and gently fold the dough.

12. Cover the dough with the tea towel again and set aside for 60 minutes.

13. Heat up an oven to 350 degrees Fahrenheit.

14. Evenly divide the dough into three portions.

15. Gently roll each of the dough portions into a 20 by 2" rope.

16. Join the top of the three rolls of dough together and pinch it together.

17. Braid the dough with the remaining part of the rolled dough.

18. Use a sheet of parchment paper to line a Dutch oven.

19. Transfer the braided dough to the lined Dutch oven (gently curve the dough to fit into the Dutch oven).

20. Place a lid on the Dutch oven and set aside for 20 minutes.

21. Place the Dutch oven on the middle rack of the preheated oven.

22. Bake the dough until lightly golden, or for 40 minutes.

23. Add the remaining ingredients to a small bowl and mix until an egg wash is formed.

24. Use the egg wash to brush the top of the baked bread.

25. Return the baked bread to the oven and bake for an additional 5–10 minutes.

26. Transfer the saffron-braided bread to a cooling rack to cool.

27. Serve the bread or wrap it in foil and store it for 2 days at a warm temperature, or transfer it to plastic bags and freeze it for 4 weeks.

Nutritional Information/Serving

Calories: 319 kcal, Protein: 7g, Fiber: 2g, Carbohydrates: 49g, Fat: 10g

26. No-Knead Baguette

Prep Time: 10 minutes

Cook Time: 35 minutes

Serves: 8 servings

Ingredients

1 1/2 cups of water

1 tablespoon of olive oil

½ tablespoon of yeast

1 ½ teaspoons of salt

1 tablespoon of sugar

4 cups of white flour

Preparation

1. Line a Dutch oven with a sheet of parchment paper and set aside.

2. In a big bowl, add the yeast, salt, sugar, and water, and mix until combined.

3. Add the white flour to the sugar mixture and mix until a dough is formed.

4. Add the olive oil to the dough and rub it until evenly coated.

5. Use a plastic wrap to cover the dough bowl and set aside for 2 hours at room temperature.

6. Gently punch down the dough in the bowl.

7. On a floured, plain surface, transfer the dough and flatten the top of the dough.

8. Evenly divide the dough into two equal portions.

9. Use a rolling pin to flatten each dough into a square shape.

10. Tightly roll each dough into a log shape.

11. Transfer the rolled dough to the lined Dutch oven.

12. Place a lid on the Dutch oven and set aside for 30–60 minutes.

13. Use bread lame to score the top of the dough.

14. Transfer the Dutch oven to an oven.

15. Bake the dough for 20–35 minutes at 400° Fahrenheit.

Nutritional Information/Serving

Calories: 942 kcal, Protein: 26g, Fiber: 7g, Carbohydrates: 197g, Fat: 3g

27. Yeast Baguette

Prep Time: 5 minutes

Cook Time: 20 minutes

Serves: 2 servings

Ingredients

96 g of water, warm

3 g of instant yeast

3 g of kosher salt

120 g of white flour (plus more for sprinkling)

Preparation

1. In a mixing bowl, add all the ingredients and stir until combined.

2. Cover the dough bowl and set it aside for 30 minutes.

3. Stretch and fold the dough with a damp hand.

4. Flip the folded dough, then transfer it to the bowl with the seam part facing down.

5. Use plastic wrap to cover the dough and set aside for 30 minutes.

6. Stretch and fold the dough again.

7. Transfer the dough with the seam facing down to the bowl again.

8. Cover the folded dough with the plastic wrap again and set aside for 60 minutes.

9. Place a lidded Dutch oven in the oven.

10. Heat up the oven to 450 degrees Fahrenheit.

11. In the dough bowl, sprinkle flour on top of the dough and turn the dough until evenly coated with the flour.

12. Shape the dough into a rectangle shape.

13. Roll the dough to form a baguette shape.

14. Use plastic wrap to cover the dough and set aside for 30 minutes.

15. Transfer the rolled dough to a sheet of parchment paper.

16. Score the top of the dough vertically and spray the dough with warm water.

17. Transfer the dough to the heated Dutch oven with the parchment paper.

18. Cover the Dutch oven with a lid and return it to the heated oven.

19. Bake the dough for 10 minutes.

20. Uncover the Dutch oven and bake the bread for 10 minutes more.

21. Transfer the baguette to a wire rack to cool, slice, and serve.

Nutritional Information/Serving

Calories: 224 kcal, Protein: 6.9g, Fiber: 2g,
Carbohydrates: 46.3g, Fat: 0.7g

Chapter 5: Sourdough Breads

28. Sourdough Rosemary Bread

Prep Time: 15 minutes

Cook Time: 45 minutes

Serves: 10 servings

Ingredients

1 tablespoon freshly chopped rosemary

20 g salt

650 g of warm water

200 g of ripe sourdough starter

250 g bread flour

200 g of whole wheat flour, freshly ground

500 g unbleached flour

Preparation

1. Add the salt, starter, warm water, and flours to a big mixing bowl and mix until combined.

2. Use plastic wrap to cover the flour mixture and set aside for 30 minutes.

3. Add the fresh rosemary to the flour mixture and mix together.

4. Stretch and fold the dough, cover, and set aside for 15 minutes twice.

5. Stretch and fold the dough again, cover, and set aside for 30 minutes twice.

6. Transfer the folded dough to a plain surface and evenly divide it into two portions.

7. Shape each of the dough portions into a round shape.

8. Set aside the shaped doughs without covering for 15 to 20 minutes.

9. Turn the dough and reshape it into a round shape.

10. Transfer the dough to a floured proofing basket and refrigerate for 12 to 15 hours.

11. For 30 minutes, place a Dutch oven in an oven and heat up the oven to 500 degrees Fahrenheit.

12. Sprinkle flour on top of the dough.

13. Use bread lame to score the dough and transfer it to a sheet of parchment paper.

14. Gently transfer the dough to the heated Dutch oven with the parchment paper.

15. Place a lid on the Dutch oven and bake the dough for 20 minutes.

16. Reduce the oven temperature to 475 degrees Fahrenheit.

17. Uncover the Dutch oven and bake the bread until golden, or for 25 minutes.

Nutritional Information/Serving

Calories: 78 kcal, Protein: 3g, Fiber: 2g, Carbohydrates: 16g, Fat: 0g

29. Pecan Sourdough Bread

Prep Time: 15 minutes

Cook Time: 1 hour

Serves: 10 servings

Ingredients

For Dough:

1/4 cup of whole wheat flour

1 ½ tsp. of Himalayan salt

4 cups of bread flour (plus extra for sprinkling)

365 g of warm water (80 degrees Fahrenheit)

1/4 cup of active sourdough starter

For Filling:

1/4 cup of coconut sugar

2 tsp. cinnamon

1/2 cup of pecans

1/3 cup of raisins

Preparation

For Dough:

1. In a big ceramic bowl, add the water and starter and mix until combined.

2. Add salt and flour to the starter mixture and mix together.

3. Use plastic wrap to cover the dough and set aside for 30 minutes.

For Filling:

4. Transfer the dough to a floured work surface and flatten the top of the dough.

5. Add the pecans and raisins to the top of the dough and knead for 1 minute.

6. Return the dough to the bowl and use plastic wrap to cover the bowl.

7. Set aside the dough at a warm temperature for 8 to 10 hours.

8. Lightly sprinkle flour on a plain surface and transfer the kneaded dough to the floured surface.

9. Set aside the dough for 10 to 15 minutes.

10. Use a tea towel to line a proofing bowl, and sprinkle flour on the towel.

11. In a bowl, add the remaining filling ingredients, stir together, and let stand.

12. Stretch the dough (with floured hands) into a rectangle shape of 8 by 16".

13. Use water to brush the top of the dough.

14. Sprinkle the sugar mixture evenly over the top of the dough (leave a 1" border around the whole corner of the dough).

15. Gently roll the filled dough into a log shape from the short edge and pinch the corners to seal the dough.

16. Transfer the shaped dough to a proofing basket with the seam side facing up.

17. Cover the basket and set aside for 30 minutes to 1 hour.

18. Place a Dutch oven with a lid in the oven.

19. Heat up the oven to 450 degrees Fahrenheit for 15 minutes.

20. Transfer the shaped dough to the middle of a sheet of parchment paper.

21. Use bread lame to score the top of the dough.

22. Transfer the dough to the hot Dutch oven with the parchment paper.

23. Place a lid on the Dutch oven and bake the dough for 20 minutes.

24. Uncover the Dutch oven and bake the bread for 40 minutes more.

25. Transfer the pecan sourdough bread to a wire cooling rack to cool, slice, and serve.

Nutritional Information/Serving

Calories: 293 kcal, Protein: 8g, Fiber: 2.9g, Carbohydrates: 55.5g, Fat: 4.6g

30. Flaxseed Sourdough Bread

Prep Time: 15 minutes

Cook Time: 35 minutes

Serves: 6 servings

Ingredients

1 ⅓ tsp. salt

4 tbsp. active sourdough starter

280 g of water

25 g of boiling water

⅛ cup of flaxseed meal

⅓ cup of whole-wheat flour

2 ⅔ cups of white bread flour

Preparation

1. In a bowl, add the sourdough starter and water, and stir until combined.

2. In another bowl, add the flaxseed meal and flours and mix until combined.

3. Add the sourdough mixture to the flour mixture and mix until combined.

4. Use plastic wrap to cover the flour mixture and set aside for 60 minutes.

5. In a small bowl, add the remaining ingredients and mix together.

6. Set aside the salt mixture to cool.

7. Add the salt mixture to the flour mixture and mix until a dough is formed.

8. Stretch and fold the dough at intervals of 30 minutes for 2 hours.

9. Shape the dough into a round shape.

10. Sprinkle flour in a proofing basket and transfer the dough to the proofing basket.

11. Use a plastic bag to cover the dough and transfer it to a refrigerator for 10 to 12 hours.

12. Remove the proofing basket from the refrigerator and set it aside for 45 minutes at room temperature.

13. Sprinkle semolina in a Dutch oven and place it in the oven.

14. Fill an ovenproof bowl with water and place the bowl in the oven too.

15. Heat up the oven to 480 degrees Fahrenheit.

16. Transfer the dough to the hot Dutch oven.

17. Use bread lame to score the dough.

18. Return the Dutch oven to the preheated oven.

19. Reduce the temperature of the oven to 428 degrees Fahrenheit (add more water to the ovenproof bowl if needed).

20. Bake the dough for 30 minutes.

21. Gently flip the bread and bake for another 5 minutes.

22. Transfer the flaxseed sourdough bread to a wire cooling rack to cool, slice, and serve.

Nutritional Information/Serving

Calories: 310 kcal, Protein: 9g, Fiber: 4g, Carbohydrates: 60g, Fat: 3g

31. Fluffy Sourdough Bread

Prep Time: 10 minutes

Cook Time: 35 minutes

Serves: 10 servings

Ingredients

Feeding Starter:

150 g water, lukewarm

150 g white flour

For Dough:

500 g bread flour

10 g of salt

350 g water, lukewarm

125 g sourdough starter

Preparation

Feeding Starter:

1. In a jar, add the water and white flour, and mix until combined.

2. Cover the jar and set aside for 6 to 8 hours at room temperature.

For Dough:

3. Add the starter and water to a big mixing bowl and mix until combined.

4. Add the flour and salt to the starter mixture and mix until a dough is formed.

5. Use plastic wrap to cover the dough and set aside for 30 minutes.

6. Stretch and fold the dough at intervals of 30 minutes for 2 hours.

7. Use plastic wrap to cover the dough and set aside for 8 to 12 hours.

8. Shape the dough into a round shape.

9. Sprinkle flour in a proofing basket and transfer the dough to the proofing basket.

10. Use plastic wrap to cover the proofing basket and refrigerate for 3 to 5 hours.

11. Place a Dutch oven with a lid in the oven.

12. Heat up the oven to 500 degrees Fahrenheit for 60 minutes.

13. Transfer the dough to a sheet of parchment paper with the seam side facing down.

14. Use bread lame to score the dough.

15. Gently transfer the dough to the hot Dutch oven with the parchment paper.

16. Place a lid on the Dutch oven and transfer it to the preheated oven.

17. Reduce the temperature of the oven to 450 degrees Fahrenheit.

18. Bake the dough for 23 minutes.

19. Uncover the Dutch oven lid and bake the bread for 12 minutes more.

20. Transfer the fluffy sourdough bread to a wire cooling rack to cool, slice, and serve.

Nutritional Information/Serving

Calories: 257 kcal, Protein: 8.3g, Fiber: 2g, Carbohydrates: 52.4g, Fat: 1.1g

32. Chocolate and Raspberry Sourdough Bread

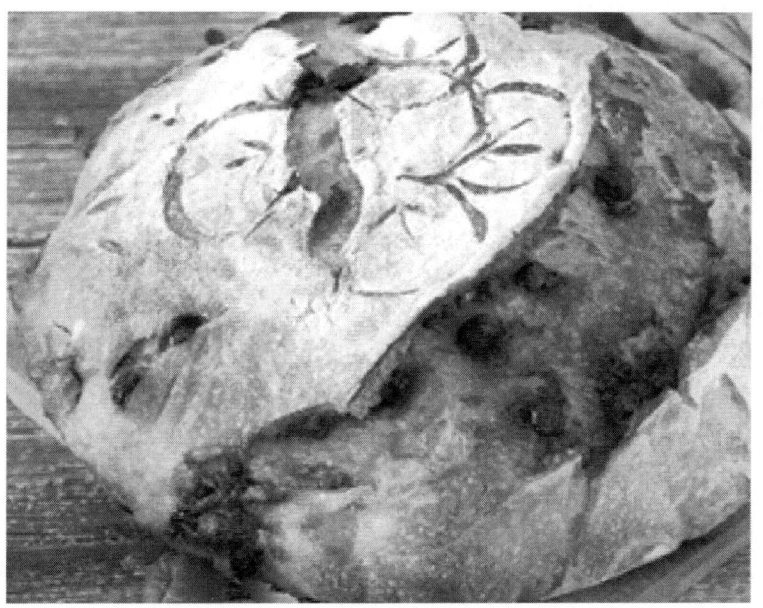

Prep Time: 10 minutes

Cook Time: 1 hour

Serves: 12 servings

Ingredients

½ cup sourdough starter

1 cup of raspberries

½ cup white chocolate chips

1 ½ cups of water

1 ¾ tsp. salt

¼ cup of rye flour

½ cups of spelt flour.

3.15 cups of bread flour

Preparation

1. Add water, rye flour, spelt flour, and bread flour to a mixing bowl and mix until combined.

2. Cover the flour mixture and set it aside for 30 minutes.

3. Add the starter to the flour mixture and mix together with your hands.

4. Knead until the dough combines, or for 1 to 2 minutes.

5. Use plastic wrap to cover the dough and set aside for 30–60 minutes.

6. Sprinkle salt over the dough and mix together.

7. Stretch and fold the dough at intervals of 1 hour for 2 hours.

8. Add the chocolate and raspberries to the dough and lightly mix together.

9. Cover the dough and set it aside for 60 minutes.

10. Lightly sprinkle flour on a plain surface, transfer the dough, and shape into a round shape.

11. Set aside the shaped dough for 15 minutes.

12. Reshape the dough and transfer it to a floured banneton with the seam side facing up.

13. Place the banneton in a refrigerator for 14 hours.

14. Heat up an oven to 475 degrees Fahrenheit.

15. Transfer the dough to a Dutch oven and place a lid on the Dutch oven.

16. Transfer the Dutch oven with the dough to the preheated oven.

17. Reduce the temperature of the oven to 450 degrees Fahrenheit.

18. Bake the dough for 25 minutes.

19. Uncover the Dutch oven and bake the bread for 35 minutes more.

20. Transfer the chocolate and raspberry bread to a cooling rack to cool, slice, and serve.

Nutritional Information/Serving

Calories: 51 kcal, Protein: 1g, Fiber: 0.1g, Carbohydrates: 7g, Fat: 2g

33. Blueberry Lime Sourdough Bread

Prep Time: 15 minutes

Cook Time: 40 minutes

Serves: 24 servings

Ingredients

1 cup of blueberries, fresh

2 big limes, zested

10 g of sea salt

320 g of water

80 g of ripe sourdough starter

70 g of whole wheat flour

100 g bread flour

230 g white flour

Preparation

1. Rinse the blueberries, use paper towels to pat them dry, and set them aside.

2. Add water and flour to a big mixing bowl and mix until combined.

3. Use plastic wrap to cover the flour mixture and set aside for 1 to 1 1/2 hours.

4. Add the ripe starter to the flour mixture and mix together.

5. Sprinkle the sea salt over the dough and mix until it combines.

6. Knead the dough until a sticky dough is formed.

7. Stretch and fold the dough, cover, and set aside for 1 hour.

8. Add the blueberries and lime zest to the dough.

9. Stretch and fold the dough again, cover, and set aside for 1 hour and 30 minutes.

10. Stretch and fold the dough, cover, and let stand for 2 hours.

11. Transfer the folded dough to a lightly floured, plain surface.

12. Shape the dough into a round shape and let it stand for 30 minutes.

13. Reshape the dough and transfer it to a lightly floured proofing basket.

14. Set aside the dough for 20 minutes without covering the basket.

15. Use plastic wrap to cover the basket and refrigerate for 14 to 16 hours.

16. In an oven, place a lidded Dutch oven and heat the oven to 500 degrees Fahrenheit.

17. Transfer the dough to the middle of a sheet of parchment paper.

18. Use bread lame to score the dough.

19. Transfer the dough to the heated Dutch oven with the parchment paper.

20. Fill a spray bottle with water and lightly spray the top of the dough.

21. Place a lid on the Dutch oven and bake the dough for 25 minutes.

22. Uncover the Dutch oven and reduce the oven temperature to 450 degrees Fahrenheit.

23. Bake the bread for 10 to 15 minutes more.

24. Transfer the blueberry lime bread to a wire cooling rack to cool, slice, and serve.

Nutritional Information/Serving

Calories: 67 kcal, Protein: 2g, Fiber: 1g, Carbohydrates: 14g, Fat: 1g

34. Walnut Cheese Sourdough Bread

Prep Time: 10 minutes

Cook Time: 43 minutes

Serves: 8 servings

Ingredients

120 g walnuts

135 g of blue cheese

60 g honey

180 g of levain

10 g salt

260 g of water

400 g of strong flour

Preparation

1. In a bowl, add water and flour, and mix until a dough is formed.

2. Set aside the flour mixture for 30 minutes at a warm temperature.

3. Add the levain, honey, and salt to the flour mixture and mix until combined.

4. Knead the dough for 2 minutes in the bowl.

5. Set aside the dough for 10 minutes.

6. Knead the dough again for a minute, and transfer to a greased bowl.

7. Set aside the dough again for 30 minutes.

8. Stretch and fold the dough, cover, and set aside for 30 minutes.

9. Add the remaining ingredients to the dough.

10. Stretch and fold the dough again, cover, and let stand for 30 minutes.

11. Stretch and fold the dough, cover, and let stand for 4 hours.

12. Transfer the folded dough to a floured, plain surface and shape the dough into a round shape.

13. Set aside the dough for 10 minutes.

14. Line a banneton with a kitchen towel and dust the towel with rice flour.

15. Reshape the dough into a round shape and sprinkle flour on top of the dough.

16. Transfer the shaped dough to the prepared banneton with the seam side facing up.

17. Place the banneton in a refrigerator for 8 hours.

18. Place a Dutch oven with a lid in the oven and heat up the oven to 464 degrees Fahrenheit.

19. Transfer the dough to the hot Dutch oven and cover with a lid.

20. Return the Dutch oven to the heated oven and bake the dough for 35 minutes.

21. Uncover the Dutch oven and bake the dough for an additional 8 minutes.

Nutritional Information/Serving

Calories: 409 kcal, Protein: 15.5g, Fiber: 5.2g, Carbohydrates: 50.5g, Fat: 16.1g

35. Chocolate Sourdough Bread

Prep Time: 15 minutes

Cook Time: 1 hour

Serves: 12 servings

Ingredients

½ cup of chocolate chips

1 ½ tsp. salt

½ cup cocoa powder

¼ cup brown sugar, packed

4 cups of bread flour

1 ½ cups warm water (100 degrees Fahrenheit)

½ cup active sourdough starter

Preparation

1. Add water and starter to a big bowl, and mix until combined.

2. Add the remaining ingredients, except the chocolate chips, to the starter mixture.

3. Mix the flour mixture until a dough is formed.

4. Use a damp tea towel to cover the dough and set it aside for 30 to 45 minutes.

5. Lightly sprinkle flour on a plain surface.

6. Transfer the dough to the floured surface.

7. Stretch and fold the dough for about 15 seconds.

8. Transfer the folded dough to the big bowl.

9. Use plastic wrap to cover the dough and set aside for 4 to 8 hours at room temperature.

10. Lightly sprinkle flour on a plain surface again.

11. Transfer the dough to the floured surface.

12. Create a well in the middle of the dough and add the chocolate to the dough.

13. Stretch and fold the dough again, and set aside for 10 to 15 minutes.

14. Line a proofing basket with a linen cover and dust with rice flour.

15. Transfer the dough to the lined basket and set aside for 45 minutes to 1 hour.

16. Heat an oven to 450 degrees Fahrenheit.

17. Transfer the dough to the middle of a 20-inch-long sheet of parchment paper.

18. Score the dough with bread lame.

19. Transfer the dough with the parchment paper to a Dutch oven.

20. Place a lid on the Dutch oven.

21. Transfer the Dutch oven to the preheated oven.

22. Bake the dough for 30 minutes.

23. Uncover the Dutch oven and bake the bread for 20 minutes more.

24. Transfer the bread to an oven rack and bake for an additional 5 to 10 minutes.

25. Gently transfer the chocolate bread to a wire cooling rack to cool, slice, and serve.

Nutritional Information/Serving

Calories: 226 kcal, Protein: 7g, Fiber: 3g, Carbohydrates: 43g, Fat: 4g

36. Seeded Sourdough Bread

Prep Time: 15 minutes

Cook Time: 50 minutes

Serves: 8 servings

Ingredients

For Seed Filling:

140 g of water (at room temperature)

20 g bulghur wheat

20 g sunflower seeds

20 g sesame seeds

20 g flax seeds

20 g chia seeds

For Dough:

9 g of salt

100 g of whole-wheat flour

400 g bread flour

100 g of levain

355 g of lukewarm water

Rice flour (for sprinkling)

Preparation

For Seed Filling:

1. Add the water and all the seeds to a bowl, stir together, and set aside for 2 hours.

For Dough:

2. In another bowl, add the flours and set aside.

3. Add the water and levain to a third bowl and stir together.

4. Add the flour mixture to the levain mixture and mix until a dough is formed.

5. Set aside the dough for 30 minutes.

6. Sprinkle the salt over the seed mixture.

7. Gently knead the dough and add the seed mixture to the dough.

8. Stretch and fold the dough with wet hands at intervals of 30 minutes for 2 hours.

9. Cover the dough and set it aside for 30 to 60 minutes.

10. Transfer the folded dough to a lightly floured work surface and shape it into a ball shape.

11. Set aside the dough for 10 minutes, and reshape the dough.

12. Sprinkle rice flour in a proofing basket.

13. Sprinkle flour on the dough and transfer it to the prepared basket.

14. Use a damp towel to cover the basket and set it aside for 2 hours and 30 minutes at a warm temperature.

15. Place a Dutch oven with a lid in the oven and heat up the oven to 475 degrees Fahrenheit.

16. Transfer the dough to the middle of a sheet of parchment paper.

17. Transfer the dough with the paper to the heated Dutch oven.

18. Lightly sprinkle flour on the dough.

19. Score the dough with bread lame and place a lid on the Dutch oven.

20. Return the Dutch oven to the heated oven.

21. Reduce the oven temperature to 450 degrees Fahrenheit.

22. Bake the dough for 25 minutes.

23. Uncover the Dutch oven and bake the bread for 25 minutes more.

24. Transfer the seeded sourdough bread to a cooling rack to cool, slice, and serve.

Nutritional Information/Serving

Calories: 297 kcal, Protein: 10g, Fiber: 5g, Carbohydrates: 52g, Fat: 6g

37. Cherry Sourdough Bread

Prep Time: 15 minutes

Cook Time: 55 minutes

Serves: 12 servings

Ingredients

For Levain:

8 g sourdough starter, ripe

84 g of water

42 g of whole-wheat flour

42 g of white flour

For Dough:

14 g salt

514 g of water

16 g caster sugar

24 g canola oil

24 g cocoa powder, unsweetened

159 g cherries, dried

159 g milk chocolate chunks

78 g of whole wheat flour

120 g of high-protein flour

516 g white flour

Preparation

For Levain:

1. Add the starter, water, and flours to a jar and mix until combined.

2. Cover the jar and set it aside for 12 hours at room temperature.

For Dough:

3. On medium heat, place a saucepan over the heat and add canola oil.

4. Cook the oil until it is warm.

5. Add the unsweetened cocoa powder to the warm oil.

6. Stir and cook the oil mixture until the mixture thickens.

7. Take the saucepan away from the heat and set it aside to cool.

8. Add 474g of water and the flours to a bowl and mix until combined.

9. Cover the flour mixture and set it aside for 30 minutes.

10. Add the levain, salt, caster sugar, and water (2 splashes) to the dough and mix together.

11. Knead the dough until a smooth dough is formed, or for 5 minutes (add water to the dough if needed).

12. Add the cocoa powder mixture to the dough and mix until combined.

13. Stretch and fold the dough, cover, and set aside for 30 minutes.

14. Add the cherries and chocolate chunks to the dough.

15. Stretch and fold the dough again at intervals of 30 minutes for 2 hours.

16. Transfer the dough to a floured, plain surface and shape into a round shape.

17. Set aside the dough for 35 minutes.

18. Reshape the dough into a round shape.

19. Transfer the dough to a banneton with the seam part facing up.

20. Cover the banneton and refrigerate for 8 hours.

21. Place a lidded Dutch oven in the oven.

22. Heat up the oven to 450 degrees Fahrenheit.

23. Transfer the dough to the middle of a sheet of parchment paper.

24. Use bread lame to score the dough top.

25. Transfer the dough to the heated Dutch oven and cover with a lid.

26. Bake the dough for 20 minutes.

27. Uncover the Dutch oven and bake for an additional 30 minutes.

28. Transfer the cherry sourdough bread to a cooling rack to cool, slice, and serve.

Nutritional Information/Serving

Calories: 346 kcal, Protein: 8.7g, Fiber: 2.7g, Carbohydrates: 59.4g, Fat: 7.1g

38. Carrot Sourdough Bread

Prep Time: 10 minutes

Cook Time: 30 minutes

Serves: 12 servings

Ingredients

Rice flour (for sprinkling)

20 g salt

200 g raisins

170 g carrots, grated

200 g of ripe sourdough starter

770 g of water (plus more for soaking)

8 cups of bread flour

Preparation

1. Fill a bowl with water and add the raisins; set aside for 8 hours.

2. Add the starter, water, and bread flour to another bowl, and mix until a dough is formed.

3. Set aside the dough for 30 minutes at a warm temperature.

4. Sprinkle salt over the dough and mix together.

5. Add the grated carrots and raisins to the dough and mix until combined.

6. Use plastic wrap to cover the dough and set aside for 30 minutes at a warm temperature.

7. Stretch and fold the dough at intervals of 30 minutes for 3 hours.

8. Evenly divide the dough into two portions.

9. Shape each dough into a round shape.

10. Sprinkle rice flour in two proofing baskets.

11. Transfer each dough to each floured basket.

12. Place the baskets in the refrigerator for 14 to 18 hours.

13. Transfer each dough to a Dutch oven and cover with a lid.

14. Transfer the Dutch ovens to an oven and bake the dough for 20 minutes at 475 degrees Fahrenheit.

15. Uncover the Dutch oven and bake the dough for 10 minutes more.

Nutritional Information/Serving

Calories: 352 kcal, Protein: 9.7g, Fiber: 4.4g, Carbohydrates: 79.5g, Fat: 0.2g

39. Roasted Beet Sourdough Bread

Prep Time: 15 minutes

Cook Time: 2 hours, 5 minutes

Serves: 12 servings

Ingredients

For Pate Fermentee:

12 g of sourdough starter

1/2 teaspoon salt

90 g of water

136 g of white flour

For Roasting Beets:

2 thyme sprigs

300 g of beets

Olive oil

For Dough:

2 tablespoons of fennel seeds

8 g salt

2 tablespoons of honey

155 g of water

66 g whole-spelt flour

40 g of rye flour, whole grain

225 g of white flour

Preparation

For Pate Fermentee:

1. In a medium bowl, add the starter, salt, water, and white flour and mix until combined.

2. Use plastic wrap to tightly cover the flour mixture.

3. Set aside the flour mixture for 12 to 16 hours at room temperature.

For Roasting Beets:

4. Use aluminum foil to line a baking sheet.

5. Place a rack in the middle of an oven and heat up the oven to 400°F.

6. Cut the beet leafy tops off and wash the beets.

7. Transfer the washed beets to the lined baking sheet.

8. Lightly drizzle oil over the beets and add the thyme sprigs.

9. Gently wrap the aluminum foil and roast for 45 minutes to 1 hour.

10. Set aside the roasted beets to cool and trim off the roots and stems.

11. Peel the beet skin and use a potato masher to mash the roasted beets.

For Dough:

12. In a bowl, add the flours, salt, honey, water, and 160g of the mashed beets.

13. Mix the flour mixture until a dough is formed.

14. Add the pate fermentee to the dough and mix until combined (add additional flour if desired).

15. Add the seeds to the dough and mix together.

16. Use bee wrap to cover the dough and set aside at room temperature for 2 to 2 hours and 30 minutes.

17. Fold the dough at intervals of 30 minutes for 1 hour and 30 minutes.

18. Lightly sprinkle flour on a work surface and transfer the dough to the surface.

19. Shape the dough into a round shape and set aside for 10–15 minutes.

20. Sprinkle flour in a lined proofing basket with a sheet of parchment paper.

21. Reshape the dough and transfer it to the prepared basket with the seam side facing up.

22. Use a tea towel to cover the basket and set it aside for 45 to 60 minutes at a warm temperature.

23. Place a Dutch oven with a lid in the oven.

24. Heat up the oven to 450 degrees Fahrenheit for 40 minutes.

25. Transfer the dough to the middle of the prepared parchment paper.

26. Use bread lame to score the dough.

27. Transfer the dough with the parchment paper to the heated Dutch oven.

28. Place a lid on the Dutch oven and bake the dough for 20 to 25 minutes.

29. Uncover the Dutch oven and bake the bread for 35 to 40 minutes.

30. Transfer the roasted beet sourdough bread to a cooling rack to cool, slice, and serve.

Nutritional Information/Serving

Calories: 336 kcal, Protein: 4.9g, Fiber: 3.3g, Carbohydrates: 37.6g, Fat: 18.9g

40. Poppy Seed Sourdough Bread

Prep Time: 15 minutes

Cook Time: 35 minutes

Serves: 12 servings

Ingredients

Rice flour (for dusting)

2 tbsp. poppy seeds

2 medium (grated) beetroots

10 g salt

375 g of water

100 g of whole-wheat flour

400 g bread flour

100 g of active sourdough starter

Preparation

1. Add the water and starter to a big mixing bowl, and mix until combined.

2. Add the flours to the starter mixture and mix until a dough is formed.

3. Set aside the dough for 30 minutes at a warm temperature.

4. Add the remaining ingredients, except the rice flour, to the dough and mix together.

5. Stretch and fold the dough at intervals of 30 minutes for 3 hours.

6. Cover the dough and set it aside at room temperature for 3 to 4 hours.

7. Use the rice flour to dust a proofing basket.

8. Transfer the dough to a lightly floured, plain surface.

9. Shape the dough into a round shape.

10. Transfer the dough to the floured basket with the seam side facing up.

11. Loosely cover the basket and refrigerate for 8 hours.

12. Place a Dutch oven with a lid in the oven.

13. Heat up the oven for 45 minutes at 450 degrees Fahrenheit.

14. Transfer the dough to the center of a sheet of parchment paper.

15. Use bread lame to score the dough.

16. Transfer the dough to the heated Dutch oven with the parchment paper.

17. Place a lid on the Dutch oven and bake the dough for 20 minutes.

18. Uncover the Dutch oven and bake the bread for 15 minutes more.

19. Leave the bread in the oven for 15 minutes.

20. Transfer the bread to a cooling rack, slice, and serve.

Nutritional Information/Serving

Calories: 176 kcal, Protein: 6g, Fiber: 3g,
Carbohydrates: 35g, Fat: 1g

41. Rainbow Sourdough Bread

Prep Time: 15 minutes

Cook Time: 40 minutes

Serves: 6 servings

Ingredients

7 g of powdered blueberry, freeze-dried

2 g of powdered butterfly pea

2 g of powdered matcha

2 g of powdered turmeric

12 g strawberry powder, freeze-dried

225g of water

1000 mg of vitamin C

6 g salt

60 g of hydrated levain

30 g of whole-wheat flour

30 g of rye flour

30 g of spelt flour

210 g of bread flour

Preparation

1. Add 210g of water and flour to a big mixing bowl and mix until a dough is formed.

2. Use plastic wrap to cover the dough and set aside for 1 hour and 30 minutes.

3. Add the levain to the dough and mix together.

4. Cover the dough and set it aside for 30 minutes.

5. Add vitamin C, salt, and the remaining water to the dough and mix until combined.

6. Evenly divide the dough into 5 portions.

7. Add the powdered blueberry to the first portion of the dough and mix until combined.

8. Add the powdered butterfly pea to the second portion of the dough and mix until combined.

9. Add the powdered matcha to the third portion of the dough and mix until combined.

10. Add the powdered turmeric to the fourth portion of the dough and mix until combined.

11. Add the strawberry powder to the fifth portion of the dough and mix until combined.

12. Cover each dough and set aside for 30 to 45 minutes.

13. Lightly bench fold each of the dough portions and let stand for 30 to 45 minutes.

14. Coil-fold each dough and let it stand for 30 to 45 minutes.

15. Spray a little water on a work surface.

16. Transfer the 5 dough portions to the work surface.

17. Laminate the dough, with each dough overlapping the other.

18. Fold up the dough and let it stand for 45 minutes to 1 hour.

19. Coil, fold the dough again, shape into a round shape, and set aside for 2 hours.

20. Reshape the dough into a round shape and transfer it to a floured proofing basket.

21. Transfer the basket to the refrigerator for 8 hours.

22. Place a lidded Dutch oven in an oven and heat up the oven to 482 degrees Fahrenheit.

23. Transfer the basket with the dough to a counter for 40 minutes.

24. Use a bread lame to score the top of the dough and transfer it to the center of a sheet of parchment paper.

25. Transfer the dough with the paper to the heated Dutch oven.

26. Place a lid on the Dutch oven and bake the dough for 20 minutes.

27. Uncover the Dutch oven and bake the bread for 10 minutes more at 428 degrees Fahrenheit.

28. Reduce the temperature of the oven again.

29. Bake the bread for 10 minutes more at 410 degrees Fahrenheit.

30. Transfer the rainbow sourdough bread to a wire cooling rack to cool, slice, and serve.

Nutritional Information/Serving

Calories: 199 kcal, Protein: 6.4g, Fiber: 2.8g, Carbohydrates: 40.6g, Fat: 1.1g

42. Apricot Sourdough Bread

Prep Time: 15 minutes

Cook Time: 50 minutes

Serves: 12 servings

Ingredients

For Levain:

80 g of water

8 g of sourdough starter, ripe

40 g of whole-wheat flour

40 g of white flour

For Main Dough:

16 g salt

611 g of water, divided

2 g lime zest

2 g of thyme, freshly minced

180 g apricots, dried

409 g of whole-wheat flour

409 g of white flour

Preparation

For Levain:

1. Add water, starter, and flour to a small bowl and mix until combined.

2. Use plastic wrap to cover the flour mixture and set aside for 12 hours at room temperature.

For Main Dough:

3. Add 548g of water and flour to a bowl and mix until a dough is formed.

4. Use plastic wrap to cover the dough and set aside for 30 minutes.

5. Add the levain, salt, and 31.5g of water to the dough and stir until combined.

6. Knead the dough until a smooth texture is formed.

7. Add 31.5g of water, lime zest, and minced thyme to the dough and mix together.

8. Stretch and fold the dough, cover it, and set aside for 30 minutes.

9. Add the dried apricots to the dough.

10. Stretch and fold the dough again, cover it, and set aside for 30 minutes.

11. Lightly sprinkle flour on a work surface, and transfer the dough to the floured surface.

12. Evenly divide the dough into two portions.

13. Shape each dough lightly into a round shape and set aside for 35 minutes.

14. Lightly sprinkle flour on top of each shaped dough.

15. Reshape the doughs and transfer them to bannetons with the seam side facing up.

16. Use plastic wrap to cover each banneton.

17. Transfer the bannetons to the refrigerator for 8 hours.

18. Place two Dutch ovens with lids in an oven.

19. Heat up the oven to 450 degrees Fahrenheit.

20. Use bread lame to score the doughs and transfer them to the hot Dutch ovens.

21. Cover the Dutch ovens with the lid and bake the dough for 20 minutes.

22. Uncover the Dutch ovens and bake the bread for 30 minutes more.

23. Transfer the loaves to a cooling rack to cool, slice, and serve.

Nutritional Information/Serving

Calories: 294 kcal, Protein: 9.9g, Fiber: 7.7g, Carbohydrates: 58.5g, Fat: 1.3g

43. Lime and Berry Sourdough Bread

Prep Time: 10 minutes

Cook Time: 45 minutes

Serves: 10 servings

Ingredients

20 g of brown sugar

Lime zest

10 g maple syrup

25 g blueberries, dried

Boiling water

10 g salt

500 g bread flour

350 g of warm water

75 g of active sourdough starter

Preparation

1. In a small bowl, add maple syrup and dried blueberries, and mix together.

2. Cover the blueberry mixture with boiling water.

3. Use cling wrap to cover the blueberry mixture and set aside for 60 minutes.

4. In another small bowl, add the sugar and lime zest, and mix together.

5. Mash the sugar mixture with a spoon and let it stand for 60 minutes.

6. In a glass bowl, add starter and warm water, and mix together.

7. Add salt and bread flour to the starter mixture and mix until a dough is formed.

8. Use a damp tea towel to cover the dough and set aside for 60 minutes.

9. Shape the dough into a round shape.

10. Stretch and fold the dough for an interval of 30 minutes for 1 hour.

11. Drain the blueberry mixture and add it to the dough.

12. Add the sugar mixture to the dough too.

13. Stretch and fold the dough again at intervals of 30 minutes for 1 hour.

14. Use a damp towel to cover the dough and set it aside for 2 hours.

15. Reshape the dough into a round shape and transfer it to a floured proofing basket.

16. Loosely cover the basket with a damp kitchen towel.

17. Transfer the basket to the refrigerator for 5 to 8 hours.

18. Place a lidded Dutch oven in the oven.

19. Heat up the oven to 450 degrees Fahrenheit for 60 minutes.

20. Transfer the dough to the center of a sheet of parchment paper.

21. Use bread lame to score the dough and transfer it to the hot Dutch oven.

22. Place a lid on the Dutch oven and bake the dough for 30 minutes.

23. Remove the Dutch oven lid.

24. Bake the bread for 10 to 15 minutes more at 390 degrees Fahrenheit.

25. Transfer the bread to a wire cooling rack to cool, slice, and serve.

Nutritional Information/Serving

Calories: 206 kcal, Protein: 6.5g, Fiber: 1.6g, Carbohydrates: 42.2g, Fat: 0.9g

44. Tasty Sourdough Bread

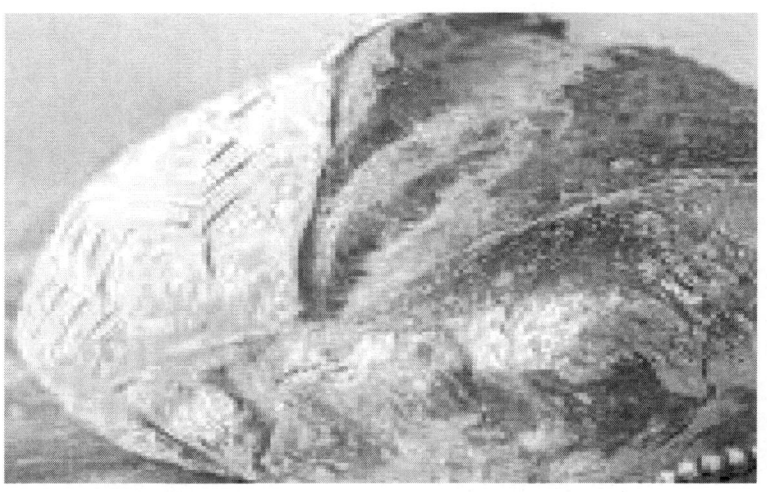

Prep Time: 15 minutes

Cook Time: 1 hour

Serves: 8 servings

Ingredients

1 tbsp. salt

1¾ cups of water

5 cups of bread flour, unbleached

1 cup of ripe sourdough starter

Preparation

1. In a big bowl, add water, bread flour, and ripe starter, and mix until a dough is formed.

2. Use plastic wrap to cover the bowl and set it aside for 20 minutes.

3. Add salt to the dough and mix together.

4. Transfer the dough to a non-reactive glass.

5. Use a damp tea towel to cover the dough and set aside for 60 minutes.

6. Transfer the dough to a plain surface.

7. Stretch and fold the dough at intervals of 1 hour for 3 hours.

8. Transfer the dough to another big bowl, cover, and refrigerate for 8 hours.

9. Set aside the dough for 1 hour on a counter.

10. Return the dough to the plain surface and shape it into a round shape.

11. Transfer the dough to the center of a sheet of parchment paper.

12. Place a Dutch oven with a lid in the oven.

13. Heat up the oven at 480 degrees Fahrenheit for 30 minutes.

14. Lightly sprinkle flour on the dough and score the dough with bread lame.

15. Transfer the dough with the paper to the heated Dutch oven.

16. Place a lid on the Dutch oven.

17. Bake the dough at 450 degrees Fahrenheit for 45 minutes.

18. Remove the Dutch oven lid and bake the bread for 10–15 minutes.

19. Transfer the bread to a cooling rack to cool.

20. Serve the bread, or tightly wrap and freeze for 12 weeks, or lightly wrap and store on a counter for 4 days.

Nutritional Information/Serving

Calories: 306 kcal, Protein: 11g, Fiber: 3g, Carbohydrates: 61g, Fat: 1g

Chapter 6: Dessert Breads

45. Honey and Milk Bread

Prep Time: 5 minutes

Cook Time: 30 minutes

Serves: 12 servings

Ingredients

1 ¾ cups of milk

3 (beaten) eggs

2 tablespoons of honey (plus more for serving)

½ cup butter, melted (plus more for serving)

¼ cup canola oil

¾ teaspoon salt

1 ½ tablespoons baking powder

1 cup of sugar

2 cups of white flour

1 cup of cornmeal

Preparation

1. In a big bowl, add the cornmeal, salt, baking powder, sugar, and flour, and mix together.

2. Add the remaining ingredients to the flour mixture and mix until combined.

3. Lightly spray a Dutch oven with nonstick cooking spray.

4. Place the sprayed Dutch oven in a brick oven.

5. Heat up the oven to 375 to 400 degrees Fahrenheit.

6. Pour the batter into the hot Dutch oven.

7. Bake the batter for 20 to 30 minutes.

8. Transfer the bread to a cooling rack to cool, slice, and serve.

Nutritional Information/Serving

Calories: 350 kcal, Protein: 6g, Fiber: 2g, Carbohydrates: 48g, Fat: 16g

46. Cinnamon Butter Bread

Prep Time: 10 minutes

Cook Time: 35 minutes

Serves: 8 servings

Ingredients

1 egg

1 1/2 cups of hot water

1/4 tsp. salt

1/2 tsp. yeast, dried

1 tsp. cinnamon

1/2 cup brown sugar

3 cups of white flour

50 g butter, melted

Preparation

1. Add all the ingredients, except the egg and water, to a big mixing bowl.

2. Mix the flour mixture until combined.

3. Gently add the water to the flour mixture and mix until a dough is formed.

4. Add the egg to the dough and mix together.

5. Use cling film to cover the dough and set aside for 3 hours.

6. Use parchment paper to line a bowl and set aside.

7. Transfer the dough to a floured, plain surface and roll the dough into a round shape.

8. Transfer the shaped dough to the prepared bowl, cover, and let stand for 40 minutes.

9. Place a lidded Dutch oven in the oven.

10. Heat up the oven to 428 degrees Fahrenheit for 30 minutes.

11. Transfer the dough to the heated Dutch oven and cover with a lid.

12. Bake the dough for 30 minutes.

13. Uncover the Dutch oven and bake the bread for an additional 5 minutes.

14. Transfer the cinnamon-butter bread to a wire cooling rack to cool, slice, and serve.

Nutritional Information/Serving

Calories: 279 kcal, Protein: 5.9g, Fiber: 1.5g, Carbohydrates: 49.8g, Fat: 6.1g

47. Nut and Cranberry Bread

Prep Time: 10 minutes

Cook Time: 35 minutes

Serves: 12 servings

Ingredients

1 1/2 cups of warm water (at 95 degrees Fahrenheit)

1 tbsp. honey

3/4 cup cranberries, dried

3/4 cup pecan nuts, chopped

1/2 tsp. yeast

2 tsp. coarse salt

3 cups plus 2 tbsp. flour (plus extra for sprinkling)

Preparation

1. In a bowl, add all the ingredients except water and mix until combined.

2. Add the warm water to the flour mixture and mix until a dough is formed.

3. Shape the dough into a round shape and return the dough to the bowl.

4. Use plastic wrap to tightly cover the dough bowl and set aside for 12–18 hours at room temperature.

5. Lightly sprinkle flour on a plain surface and transfer the dough to the surface.

6. Reshape the dough and transfer it to a sheet of parchment paper.

7. Transfer the dough with the paper to another bowl, cover it, and let it stand.

8. Use bread lame to score the top of the dough.

9. Lightly cover the dough with a towel and set aside for 30 minutes.

10. Place a lidded Dutch oven in the oven.

11. Heat up the oven to 475 degrees Fahrenheit for 30 minutes.

12. Transfer the dough to the heated Dutch oven and cover with a lid.

13. Bake the dough for 25 minutes.

14. Remove the lid of the Dutch oven and bake the bread until brown, or for an additional 8 to 10 minutes.

15. Transfer the nut and cranberry bread to a cooling rack to cool for about 20 minutes, slice, and serve.

Nutritional Information/Serving

Calories: 210 kcal, Protein: 4.1g, Fiber: 2.2g, Carbohydrates: 35.7g, Fat: 5.8g

48. Chocolate Yeast Bread

Prep Time: 10 minutes

Cook Time: 45 minutes

Serves: 8 servings

Ingredients

1 1/2 cups of water (at room temperature)

1 cup of chocolate milk chips

1/2 tsp. instant yeast

1 1/2 tsp. salt

2 tbsp. sugar, granulated

1/4 cup of cocoa powder

2 3/4 cups of bread flour

Preparation

1. In a big bowl, add all the ingredients except water, milk, and chocolate chips, and mix until combined.

2. Add the remaining ingredients to the flour mixture and mix until a dough is formed.

3. Use plastic wrap to cover the dough bowl and set aside for 18–24 hours at room temperature.

4. Transfer the dough to a sheet of parchment paper.

5. Knead the dough and shape it into a round shape.

6. Use plastic wrap to cover the dough and set it aside for 2 hours on the counter.

7. Place a Dutch oven in an oven.

8. Heat up the oven to 450 °F for 30 minutes.

9. Transfer the shaped dough to the heated Dutch oven with the parchment paper.

10. Place a lid on the Dutch oven and bake the dough for 30 minutes.

11. Uncover the Dutch oven and bake the bread for an additional 15 minutes.

Nutritional Information/Serving

Calories: 194 kcal, Protein: 6.3g, Fiber: 2.1g, Carbohydrates: 39.7g, Fat: 1.5g

49. Oat Maple Bread

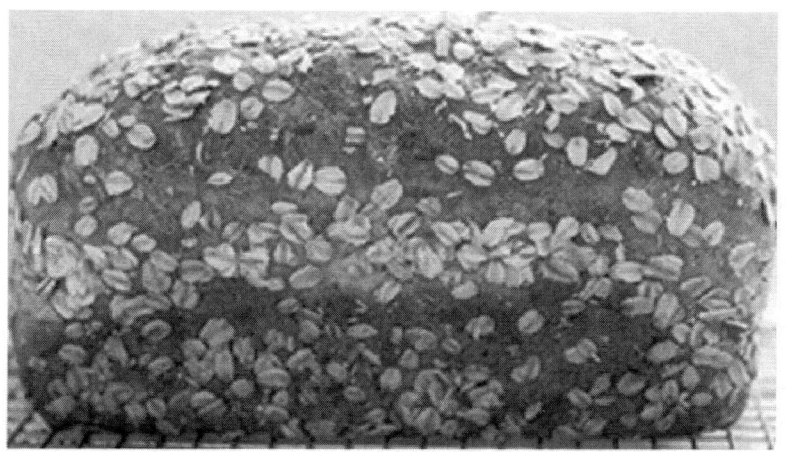

Prep Time: 10 minutes

Cook Time: 45 minutes

Serves: 8 servings

Ingredients

1 tbsp. olive oil

Unsalted soft butter (to grease)

1 cup whole-wheat flour

2¼ cups bread flour, unbleached

1 1/2 tsp. yeast

3/4 cup water (at room temperature)

1 1/2 tsp. kosher salt

¼ cup maple syrup

1 cup water, boiling

1 1/2 cups of rolled oats, divided

Preparation

1. Add the 1 cup of oats, salt, maple syrup, and boiling water to a big bowl and mix until combined.

2. Set aside the oat mixture for 10 minutes.

3. Add the 3/4 cup of water and yeast to the oat mixture and mix until combined.

4. Add the whole-wheat flour and bread flour to the oat mixture and mix until a dough is formed.

5. Gently knead the dough until a smooth texture is formed.

6. Add the remaining oats to the dough and mix together.

7. Use a kitchen towel to cover the dough and set aside for 2-3 hours at room temperature.

8. Heat up an oven to 375 degrees Fahrenheit.

9. Grease a Dutch oven with soft butter.

10. Coat the dough with the olive oil and shape into a round shape.

11. Transfer the shaped dough to the greased Dutch oven with the seam side facing down.

12. Set aside the dough for 45 minutes at room temperature.

13. Transfer the Dutch oven to the preheated oven and bake the dough for 45 minutes.

14. Transfer the bread to a wire rack to cool, slice, and serve.

Nutritional Information/Serving

Calories: 294 kcal, Protein: 8.9g, Fiber: 4.6g, Carbohydrates: 55.6g, Fat: 3.6g

50. Double Chocolate Bread

Prep Time: 10 minutes

Cook Time: 45 minutes

Serves: 8 servings

Ingredients

1 cup of chocolate chunks

1 1/2 cups plus 2 tablespoons of warm water

1/2 teaspoon dry active yeast

1 teaspoon salt

2 tablespoons of sugar

1/4 cup cocoa powder, unsweetened

3 cups of white flour

Preparation

1. Add all the ingredients except water to a big bowl and mix until combined.

2. Add the water to the flour mixture and mix until a dough is formed.

3. Use plastic wrap to cover the dough and set aside for 3 to 5 hours.

4. In an oven, place a lidded Dutch and heat up the oven to 450 degrees Fahrenheit for 30 minutes.

5. Transfer the dough to a floured work surface.

6. Stretch and fold the dough four times, and tightly shape the dough into a round shape.

7. Line a bowl with a sheet of parchment paper.

8. Gently transfer the shaped dough to the prepared bowl.

9. Use a tea towel to cover the dough and set aside for 20 minutes.

10. Transfer the dough to the heated Dutch oven with the parchment paper.

11. Use bread lame to score the top of the dough.

12. Cover the Dutch oven with a lid, and bake the dough for 30 minutes.

13. Remove the lid of the Dutch oven and bake the bread for 15 minutes more.

14. Transfer the bread to a cooling rack to cool, slice, and serve.

Nutritional Information/Serving

Calories: 348 kcal, Protein: 7.3g, Fiber: 6.2g, Carbohydrates: 54.4g, Fat: 12.8g

51. Sugar Bread with Frosting

Prep Time: 10 minutes

Cook Time: 15 minutes

Serves: 8 servings

Ingredients

For Bread:

2 teaspoons cinnamon, ground

1/2 cup sugar, granulated

1/4 cup butter, melted

2 big biscuit doughs, cut into 2cm cubes

For Frosting:

1 cup sugar, powdered

1 tablespoon of milk

2 tablespoons of soft cream cheese

Preparation

For Bread:

1. Make a campfire with enough coals.

2. Add cinnamon and sugar to a medium bowl and mix together.

3. Add the melted butter to another bowl.

4. Dunk the cubed dough in the butter and roll in the sugar mixture.

5. Line a Dutch oven with a sheet of parchment paper.

6. Transfer the coated dough to the prepared Dutch oven.

7. Place 5 coals below the Dutch oven and cover with a lid.

8. Place 14 coals on top of the Dutch oven and bake the dough for 10 to 15 minutes.

For Frosting:

9. Add all the ingredients to a bowl and mix until combined.

10. Drizzle the frosting over the sugar bread and serve.

Nutritional Information/Serving

Calories: 248 kcal, Protein: 1.4g, Fiber: 0.6g, Carbohydrates: 45.7g, Fat: 7.6g

52. Butter and Honey Bread

Prep time: 10 minutes

Cook time: 45 minutes

Serves: 8 servings

Ingredients

1/2 tsp. vanilla extract

1/2 cup honey

1/2 cup soft butter

Olive oil

1 tsp. salt

1 tsp. dry yeast

1 1/2 cups of water

4 cups of white flour

Preparation

1. Combine yeast, salt, water, and white flour in a mixing bowl.

2. Use a dough hook to blend everything at a moderate speed until your dough turns elastic.

3. Once it's well-blended and smooth, test its stretchiness by pulling a piece. It should stretch until it is transparent. If not, simply mix a bit more until you achieve the desired elasticity.

4. After mixing, set aside the mixer and use a plastic wrap or towel to cover the bowl. Let the dough double in size and rise, which usually takes 2 to 4 hours.

5. Check on it at the 2-hour mark. If the dough has doubled and doesn't bounce back when touched, it's good to go. If it does bounce back, give it some more time to rise.

6. Transfer the dough to a plain surface, knead, and shape into a round shape.

7. Use a kitchen towel to cover the dough and set it aside for 10 minutes.

8. Grease a Dutch oven.

9. Reshape the dough into a tight, round shape.

10. Transfer the shaped dough to the greased Dutch oven and cover with a lid.

11. Set aside the dough for 30 to 60 minutes.

12. Heat up the oven to 450° Fahrenheit.

13. Generously coat the dough with the oil.

14. Use bread lame to score the dough and transfer the Dutch oven to the preheated oven.

15. Bake the dough for 30 minutes.

16. Reduce the oven temperature to 375° Fahrenheit and bake the bread for 10 to 15 minutes.

17. In a small bowl, add vanilla extract, honey, and butter, and mix until combined.

18. Transfer the butter and honey bread to a wire cooling rack to cool, slice, and serve with the butter mixture.

Nutritional Information/Serving

Calories: 358 kcal, Protein: 6.5g, Fiber: 1.7g,
Carbohydrates: 65.2g, Fat: 8.3g

Chapter 7: Veggies Breads

53. Zucchini Bread

Prep Time: 10 minutes

Cook Time: 1 hour

Serves: 12 servings

Ingredients

1/2 cup nuts, roughly chopped

1/2 tsp. baking powder

1/2 tsp. cloves, ground

1 tsp. cinnamon, ground

1 tsp. salt

2 tsp. baking soda

3 cups pastry flour, whole-wheat

4 eggs

2 tsp. vanilla extract, pure

2/3 cup melted butter (plus more for greasing)

1 1/2 cups of coconut sugar

3 cups of shredded zucchini

Preparation

1. Place a Dutch oven with a lid in the oven.

2. Heat up the oven to 350 degrees Fahrenheit.

3. Use butter to grease the Dutch oven.

4. In a big bowl, add eggs, vanilla extract, butter, coconut sugar, and zucchini, and mix together.

5. Add the remaining ingredients and stir until combined.

6. Transfer the dough to the heated Dutch oven.

7. Place a lid on the Dutch oven and bake the dough for 50–60 minutes.

8. Transfer the bread to a cooling rack to cool, slice, and serve.

Nutritional Information/Serving

Calories: 375 kcal, Protein: 6.8g, Fiber: 3.6g, Carbohydrates: 55.9g, Fat: 15.6g

54. Easy Mushroom Bread

Prep Time: 15 minutes

Cook Time: 1 hour

Serves: 8 servings

Ingredients

Butter

Ground pepper

Kosher salt

1 tbsp. thyme, minced

1/4 cup flat leaf parsley, coarsely chopped

1/2 cup parmesan cheese, grated

1 1/2 cups heavy cream

2 1/2 cups of whole milk

1 cup shredded Gruyere cheese

6 big eggs

1 1/2 lb. mixed mushrooms, sliced

1 big, clean leek, diced

12 oz. of thick-cut bacon, diced

1 loaf of day-old French bread, cut into small pieces

Preparation

1. Preheat an oven to 350°F.

2. In a skillet, add the bacon and sauté until it is lightly crisp.

3. Transfer the cooked bacon to a medium bowl and set aside.

4. Add the diced leek to the skillet and sauté for 4 minutes or until soft.

5. Transfer the cooked leek to the bacon bowl and set aside.

6. Add the sliced mushrooms to the skillet and sauté until brown (you can cook this in batches).

7. Transfer the cooked mushrooms to the bacon bowl.

8. Add the ground pepper, salt, eggs, thyme, parsley, parmesan, heavy cream, and milk to another bowl and mix until combined.

9. Add the bread and bacon mixture to the milk mixture and mix together.

10. Set aside the bread mixture for 15 minutes.

11. Grease a Dutch oven with butter.

12. Transfer the bread mixture to the greased Dutch oven.

13. Sprinkle the shredded cheese over the bread mixture.

14. Bake for 45 minutes in the preheated oven.

15. Top the mushroom bread with chopped parsley and serve.

Nutritional Information/Serving

Calories: 426 kcal, Protein: 20.6g, Fiber: 4.2g, Carbohydrates: 12.5g, Fat: 32.8g

55. Buttermilk and Zucchini Bread

Prep Time: 10 minutes

Cook Time: 30 minutes

Serves: 8 servings

Ingredients

1 1/2 tbsp. shredded zucchini

Jam

1 (15-ounce) can of cream-style corn

1 cup of buttermilk

2 big (beaten) eggs

1 tsp. salt

1 tbsp. sugar

1/2 tsp. baking soda

2 tsp. baking powder

2 cups of cornmeal

Preparation

1. Grease a 10-inch Dutch oven with olive oil cooking spray.

2. Place the Dutch oven in an oven, and heat up the oven to 350° Fahrenheit.

3. Add the corn, buttermilk, and eggs to a bowl and mix until combined.

4. Add the remaining ingredients except jam to the buttermilk mixture.

5. Mix the buttermilk mixture until combined.

6. Transfer the batter to the greased Dutch oven and place a lid on it.

7. Bake the batter for 30 minutes or until brown.

8. Transfer the buttermilk bread to a wire rack to cool, slice, and serve with jam.

Nutritional Information/Serving

Calories: 196 kcal, Protein: 6g, Fiber: 4g, Carbohydrates: 32g, Fat: 5g

56. No-Knead Tomato Bread

Prep Time: 10 minutes

Cook Time: 50 minutes

Serves: 8 servings

Ingredients

4 ounces of shredded mozzarella cheese

1 tablespoon of tomato paste

1 1/2 cups of water, warm

1/2 tablespoon basil, dried

1/2 teaspoon salt

2 teaspoons instant yeast

3 cups of white flour

1/3 cup of sun-dried tomatoes, chopped

Preparation

1. Add the sun-dried tomatoes, basil, salt, yeast, and white flour to a big bowl and mix until combined.

2. Add the shredded cheese to the flour mixture and stir together.

3. In another bowl, add the water and tomato paste and mix until combined.

4. Add the tomato paste mixture to the flour mixture and mix until a dough is formed.

5. Loosely cover the dough and let it stand for 60 minutes.

6. Sprinkle flour on a work surface, and transfer the dough to the floured surface.

7. Fold the dough until a smooth texture is achieved.

8. Transfer the dough to the middle of a sheet of parchment paper.

9. Set aside the dough for 60 minutes at room temperature.

10. Heat up an oven to 425 degrees Fahrenheit.

11. Place a Dutch oven with a lid in the preheated oven for 30 minutes.

12. Transfer the dough with the paper to the heated Dutch oven.

13. Cover the Dutch oven with a lid, and bake the dough for 30 minutes.

14. Uncover the Dutch oven and bake the bread for 15 to 20 minutes more.

Nutritional Information/Serving

Calories: 237 kcal, Protein: 10g, Fiber: 3g, Carbohydrates: 40g, Fat: 4g

57. Avocado Bread

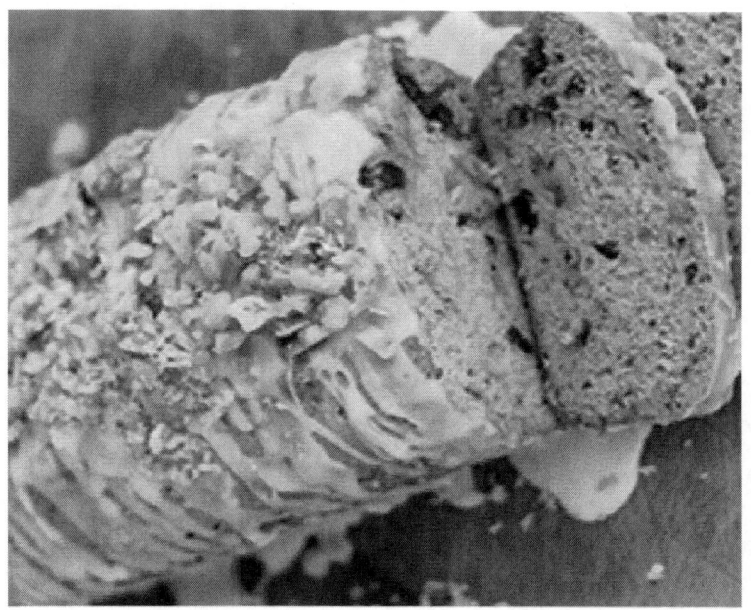

Prep Time: 10 minutes

Cook Time: 40 minutes

Serves: 6 servings

Ingredients

1 tsp. lemon juice

½ cup (mashed) avocado

¼ tsp. vanilla extract

1 egg

¼ cup butter (at room temperature)

½ cup sugar

Salt

¼ tsp. cinnamon

½ tsp. baking soda

½ teaspoon baking powder

1 cup of white flour

Preparation

1. Heat up an oven to 325° Fahrenheit.

2. Spray a Dutch oven with olive oil cooking spray.

3. Add salt, cinnamon, baking soda, baking powder, and white flour to a medium bowl and mix until combined.

4. Add the butter and sugar to another bowl and mix until fluffy.

5. Add the vanilla extract and egg to the sugar mixture and mix until combined.

6. Add the remaining ingredients to the sugar mixture and mix until combined.

7. Gently add the flour mixture to the sugar mixture and mix until just combined.

8. Transfer the flour mixture to the prepared Dutch oven and bake for 35 to 40 minutes.

Nutritional Information/Serving

Calories: 180 kcal, Protein: 20g, Fiber: 8g, Carbohydrates: 204g, Fat: 62g

58. Carrot and Seed Bread

Prep Time: 10 minutes

Cook Time: 1 hour, 5 minutes

Serves: 24 servings

Ingredients

1 tablespoon of hemp seeds

1 tablespoon of flaxseeds

1 tablespoon of sesame seeds

1 tablespoon of poppy seeds

1 tablespoon of sunflower seeds

320 ml of water, lukewarm

1 teaspoon agave syrup

6 tablespoons of chopped nuts

1 small piece of ginger, grated

2 ½ teaspoons of salt

7 g of dry yeast

2 ½ cups of wheat flour

3 ⅓ cups of whole-spelt flour

6.3 ounces of grated carrots

8.5 ounces of carrots

Preparation

1. Add the 8.5 ounces of carrots to a microwaveable bowl.

2. Place the bowl in the microwave and sauté for 15 minutes.

3. Transfer the cooked carrot to a blender and blend until a smooth texture is formed.

4. Add the salt, yeast, and flour to a big mixing bowl and mix until combined.

5. Add agave syrup, nuts, grated ginger, and grated carrots and pureed carrots to the flour mixture, and mix until combined.

6. Add water to the flour mixture and knead until a dough is formed for 5 minutes.

7. Use plastic wrap to cover the dough and set aside for 60 minutes at room temperature.

8. Lightly knead the dough again and shape it into a round shape.

9. Line a banneton with a sheet of parchment paper.

10. Transfer the dough to the lined banneton with the seam side down, and set aside for 30 minutes.

11. Place a Dutch oven with a lid in the oven.

12. Heat up the oven to 450 degrees Fahrenheit.

13. Gently use water to brush the top of the dough.

14. Sprinkle the remaining ingredients on top of the dough.

15. Transfer the dough to the heated Dutch oven with the parchment paper.

16. Place a lid on the Dutch oven and bake the dough for 35 minutes.

17. Uncover the Dutch oven and bake the bread for 15 minutes more.

Nutritional Information/Serving

Calories: 145.6 kcal, Protein: 5.1g, Fiber: 4.7g, Carbohydrates: 24.2g, Fat: 2.6g

59. Sweet Potato Bread

Prep Time: 10 minutes

Cook Time: 55 minutes

Serves: 16 servings

Ingredients

2 cups of peeled and chopped sweet potato

2 tablespoons of vanilla extract

2 tablespoons of pumpkin spice

1/2 teaspoon salt

1 tablespoon of coconut sugar

1 teaspoon of yeast

4 cups of white flour

2 cups of milk

Preparation

1. On high heat, place a big pot and add the pumpkin spice, vanilla extract, and milk.

2. Bring the milk mixture to a boil.

3. Add the chopped sweet potato to the pot and sauté until soft.

4. Remove the cooked potato and set it aside to cool.

5. Set aside 1 2/3 of the potato liquid.

6. Transfer the cooked potato to a food processor and process until a smooth texture is reached.

7. Add coconut sugar, salt, yeast, pureed potato, and the potato liquid to a big bowl and mix until combined.

8. Add the white flour to the sugar mixture and mix until a dough is formed.

9. On a floured, plain surface, transfer the dough and knead until a smooth texture is formed.

10. Return the dough to the big bowl, cover, and set aside for 8 hours at room temperature.

11. Place a Dutch oven with a lid in the oven.

12. Heat up the oven to 475° Fahrenheit.

13. Return the dough to the floured plain surface and knead again (sprinkle flour on the dough if needed).

14. Use olive oil cooking spray to spray the hot Dutch oven.

15. Transfer the dough to the sprayed Dutch oven and cover with a lid.

16. Bake the dough for 30 minutes.

17. Transfer the dough to the oven rack and bake for 20 minutes more.

18. Transfer the sweet potato bread to a wire cooling rack to cool, slice, and serve.

Nutritional Information/Serving

Calories: 170 kcal, Protein: 4.9g, Fiber: 1.5g, Carbohydrates: 31.6g, Fat: 2g

60. Tasty Onion Bread

Prep Time: 10 minutes

Cook Time: 1 hour, 15 minutes

Serves: 10 servings

Ingredients

Semolina flour (for sprinkling)

1½ cups of water

¼ tsp. dry yeast

1 tsp. salt

4 cups of flour (plus more for dusting)

1 tsp. sugar, granulated

2 tbsp. olive oil

3 big onions, peeled and sliced thinly

Preparation

1. On medium-high heat, place a big skillet over the heat and add oil.

2. Add the sliced onions to the hot oil and mix until the onion is evenly coated.

3. Sprinkle the granulated sugar over the onions in the skillet.

4. Saute the onion mixture for 30 minutes or until the onions turn brown (stir the mixture occasionally).

5. In a heatproof dish, transfer the cooked onion mixture and set aside to cool.

6. Add the yeast, salt, flour, and onion mixture to a big bowl and stir together.

7. Add water to the flour mixture and mix until a sticky dough is formed.

8. Use plastic wrap to cover the dough and set aside for 18–24 hours at room temperature.

9. Transfer the dough to the middle of a piece of floured parchment paper.

10. Sprinkle flour on top of the dough and fold the dough a few times over itself.

11. Shape the dough into a round shape.

12. Lightly dust the big bowl with flour and return the shaped dough to the bowl.

13. Use plastic wrap to cover the dough and set aside for 2 hours.

14. Place a Dutch oven with a lid in the oven.

15. Heat up the oven to 450 degrees Fahrenheit.

16. Sprinkle the semolina flour in the hot Dutch oven and transfer the dough.

17. Place a lid on the Dutch oven and bake the dough for 30 minutes.

18. Uncover the Dutch oven and bake the dough for 15 minutes more.

19. Transfer the onion bread to a cooling rack to cool, slice, and serve.

Nutritional Information/Serving

Calories: 221 kcal, Protein: 5.2g, Fiber: 1.6g, Carbohydrates: 41.3g, Fat: 3.2g

61. Healthy Artichoke Bread

Prep Time: 10 minutes

Cook Time: 35 minutes

Serves: 10 servings

Ingredients

1 cup of shredded cheddar cheese

1 (14 oz.) can of drained artichokes, quartered

2 tbsp. lemon pepper

1 tbsp. parsley

2 cups of shredded Monterey Jack cheese

1/4 cup of parmesan cheese

1 1/2 cups of sour cream

2 tbsp. sesame seeds

3 garlic cloves

1/2 cup of butter, soft

2 loaves of French bread, sliced lengthwise

Preparation

1. Remove the middle of the sliced bread and leave the shell (the bread will look like the shape of a canoe).

2. Reserve the scooped-out part (the bread pieces) of the bread.

3. Add butter to a Dutch oven and place over heat.

4. Add sesame seeds and garlic to the hot butter and cook.

5. Add the set-aside, scooped-out bread to the sesame seed mixture and stir until evenly coated.

6. Add the remaining ingredients, except the shaped bread and cheddar cheese, to another bowl and mix together.

7. Add the cooked bread mixture to the cheese mixture and mix together.

8. Gently spoon the cheese mixture into the bread shells and top with the shredded cheddar cheese.

9. Bake the bread for 30 minutes at 350° Fahrenheit.

Nutritional Information/Serving

Calories: 392 kcal, Protein: 11g, Fiber: 1.3g, Carbohydrates: 8.1g, Fat: 33.9g

62. Beetroot Bread

Prep Time: 10 minutes

Cook Time: 50 minutes

Serves: 8 servings

Ingredients

½ cup olive oil

3 teaspoons of salt

7 cups of white flour (plus more for dusting)

1 teaspoon of food coloring

2 ½ cups of warm beetroot juice

1 tablespoon runny honey

10 g instant yeast

Preparation

1. In a bowl, add the beetroot juice, honey, yeast, and food coloring, and mix together.

2. Set aside the beetroot juice mixture for 5 to 8 minutes.

3. Add salt and white flour to a large mixing bowl and mix until combined.

4. Gently pour the beetroot juice mixture and olive oil into the flour mixture.

5. Mix the flour mixture until a dough is formed.

6. Transfer the dough to a floured, plain surface and knead until a smooth dough is formed.

7. Transfer the dough to a sprayed bowl, cover it, and set aside for 2 hours.

8. Place a lidded Dutch oven in an oven.

9. Heat up the oven to 482 degrees Fahrenheit for 30 minutes.

10. Shape the dough into a round shape.

11. Sprinkle flour on top of the dough and use a bread lame to score the top of the dough.

12. Dust the heated Dutch oven with flour.

13. Transfer the dough to the hot Dutch oven, cover with a lid, and bake the dough for 30 minutes.

14. Reduce the oven temperature to 428 degrees Fahrenheit and bake the bread for 20 minutes more.

Nutritional Information/Serving

Calories: 289 kcal, Protein: 5.4g, Fiber: 0.5g, Carbohydrates: 69.3g, Fat: 14.4g

63. Irish Potato No-Knead Bread

Prep Time: 10 minutes

Cook Time: 1 hour, 10 minutes

Serves: 16 servings

Ingredients

2 tsp. salt

4½ cups of white flour

1 tbsp. active dry yeast

2 cups water, warm

Cold water

12 oz. of Irish potatoes, cut into bite-size pieces

Preparation

1. In a big pot, add the cold water, a teaspoon of salt, and the potatoes (the water should cover the Irish potatoes).

2. Stir the potato mixture together.

3. Place the pot over high heat and bring the potato mixture to a boil.

4. Reduce the flame to medium and sauté the potato mixture until soft, or for 15 minutes.

5. Drain the cooked Irish potatoes and mash them with a potato masher.

6. Set aside the mashed potato to cool.

7. Add the flour, yeast, salt, and mashed potatoes to a large bowl and mix together.

8. Add the warm water to the flour mixture and mix until a dough is formed.

9. Use plastic wrap to cover the dough and set aside for 60 minutes.

10. Place a lidded Dutch oven in an oven and heat up the oven to 450 degrees Fahrenheit.

11. Place the dough on a floured, plain surface and shape the dough into a round shape with floured hands.

12. Transfer the shaped dough to the middle of a piece of parchment paper.

13. Transfer the dough with the paper to the heated Dutch oven and cover with a lid.

14. Bake the dough for 30 minutes.

15. Uncover the Dutch oven and bake the bread until brown, or for 15-20 minutes more.

Nutritional Information/Serving

Calories: 145 kcal, Protein: 4g, Fiber: 1g, Carbohydrates: 31g, Fat: 0.4g

64. Simple Cabbage Bread

Prep Time: 10 minutes

Cook Time: 40 minutes

Serves: 10 servings

Ingredients

2 (10 oz.) cans of refrigerated biscuits

1/8 tsp. of pepper

1/2 tsp. salt

2 cups of sliced onions, cut in half

4 cups of chopped cabbage

1/2 cup of butter

Preparation

1. Heat up an oven to 375 degrees Fahrenheit.

2. Place a Dutch oven over heat and add butter.

3. Add pepper, salt, onion, and chopped cabbage to the hot butter and mix together.

4. Place a lid on the Dutch oven.

5. Saute the cabbage mixture until soft and crisp, or for 10 to 15 minutes on medium heat (occasionally stir the cabbage mixture).

6. Gently separate the refrigerated biscuits into 20 equal portions.

7. Press over the bottom of the dough and the" 1/2"-up parts of a 9 by 13 pan.

8. Spoon the cooked cabbage mixture over the dough.

9. Bake the dough until brown, or for 18 to 25 minutes.

Nutritional Information/Serving

Calories: 207 kcal, Protein: 4g, Fiber: 1.6g, Carbohydrates: 25.1g, Fat: 10.2g

65. Artisan Potato Bread

Prep Time: 10 minutes

Cook Time: 40 minutes

Serves: 8 servings

Ingredients

2 cups of sharp cheddar cheese, shredded

3/4 cup potato flakes, dried

1 3/4 cups of water, warm

2 teaspoons of salt

1/2 teaspoon active yeast

3 cups of white flour

Preparation

1. Add all the ingredients except cheese to a big bowl and mix for 20 seconds.

2. Add the shredded cheese to the flour mixture and mix until a dough is formed.

3. Use plastic wrap to cover the dough and set aside for 8 to 12 hours at room temperature.

4. Transfer the dough to a floured, plain surface and shape into a round shape.

5. Transfer the dough to the middle of a sheet of parchment paper.

6. Set aside the dough at a warm temperature for 20 to 30 minutes.

7. Place a lidded Dutch oven in an oven.

8. Preheat the oven for 20 to 30 minutes at 450 degrees Fahrenheit.

9. Use bread lame to score the top of the dough.

10. Transfer the dough to the heated Dutch oven with the paper.

11. Cover the Dutch oven with a lid, and bake the dough for 25 minutes.

12. Uncover the Dutch oven and bake the bread at 425 degrees Fahrenheit for 10 to 15 minutes.

Nutritional Information/Serving

Calories: 82.5 kcal, Protein: 6.6g, Fiber: 1.4g, Carbohydrates: 2.9g, Fat: 5.1g

66. Broccoli Cheese Bread

Prep Time: 5 minutes

Cook Time: 32 minutes

Serves: 6 servings

Ingredients

Butter

1 teaspoon salt

2 teaspoons baking powder

4 tablespoons of coconut flour

3/4 cup of raw and chopped broccoli florets

1 cup of cheddar cheese, shredded

5 whisked eggs

Preparation

1. Heat up an oven to 350 degrees Fahrenheit.

2. Grease a Dutch oven with butter.

3. In a big bowl, add salt, baking powder, broccoli, cheese, eggs, and flour.

4. Mix the cheese mixture until combined.

5. Transfer the cheese mixture to the prepared Dutch oven.

6. Bake the cheese mixture until brown, or for 28 to 32 minutes.

Nutritional Information/Serving

Calories: 116 kcal, Protein: 7.8g, Fiber: 1.9g, Carbohydrates: 4.6g, Fat: 7.6g

67. Cucumber Bread

Prep Time: 10 minutes

Cook Time: 1 hour

Serves: 12 servings

Ingredients

1/2 cup of pecans, chopped

1/4 tsp. cloves, ground

1/4 tsp. nutmeg

1/4 tsp. baking powder

1 tsp. salt

1 tsp. baking soda

1 1/2 cups of flour

1 tsp. lime juice

1 tsp. of vanilla extract

1 cup peeled cucumber, deseeded, grated, and drained

1 cup of sugar

1/2 cup of vegetable oil

2 eggs

Preparation

1. Heat up an oven to 350° Fahrenheit.

2. Add sugar, oil, and eggs to a big bowl and mix together.

3. Add lime juice, vanilla, and cucumber to the oil mixture and stir together.

4. Add the remaining ingredients, except pecans, to the oil mixture and mix until combined.

5. Add the chopped pecans to the oil mixture and mix together.

6. Use a nonstick cooking spray to spray a Dutch oven.

7. Add the batter to the sprayed Dutch oven and bake for 1 hour.

8. Transfer the cucumber bread to a wire cooling rack to cool, slice, and serve.

Nutritional Information/Serving

Calories: 247 kcal, Protein: 3.1g, Fiber: 0.9g, Carbohydrates: 29.7g, Fat: 13.4g

Chapter 8: Fruit Breads

68. Easy Strawberry Bread

Prep Time: 10 minutes

Cook Time: 1 hour

Serves: 8 servings

Ingredients

2 cups of strawberries, chopped

1/2 cup of sour cream

1 (beaten) egg

2 teaspoons of vanilla extract

1 cup of sugar

3 ounces of soft cream cheese

1 teaspoon salt

1 teaspoon baking soda

2 cups of white flour

Preparation

1. Heat up an oven to 350 degrees Fahrenheit.

2. In a big bowl, add salt, baking soda, and white flour, mix together, and let stand.

3. Add vanilla, cream cheese, sugar, and egg to another bowl and mix until combined.

4. Add the flour mixture to the sugar mixture and mix until just combined.

5. Add the sour cream to the batter and mix lightly.

6. Add the strawberries to the batter and mix together.

7. Spray a Dutch oven with nonstick cooking spray.

8. Transfer the batter to the sprayed Dutch oven and bake for 55 minutes to 1 hour.

9. Transfer the strawberry bread to a wire cooling rack to cool, slice, and serve.

Nutritional Information/Serving

Calories: 304 kcal, Protein: 5.5g, Fiber: 1.7g, Carbohydrates: 54.1g, Fat: 7.3g

69. Mixed Fruit Bread

Prep Time: 15 minutes

Cook Time: 1 hour, 5 minutes

Serves: 12 servings

Ingredients

3 cups of bread flour

2 packets of instant yeast

1 1/2 teaspoons of allspice, ground

1 1/2 teaspoons of cinnamon, ground

1 teaspoon salt

1/4 cup of light brown sugar

2 medium (whisked) eggs

110g of butter, unsalted

3/4 cup of milk

1/2 cup plus 2 tablespoons of black tea, hot

1 1/3 cups of dried mixed fruit

3/4 cup of chopped prunes

Preparation

1. In a bowl, add the hot black tea and mixed fruit, and set aside to soak.

2. Place a skillet over heat and add the unsalted butter.

3. Add the milk to the hot butter and cook until just warm.

4. Add the sugar and eggs to another bowl and mix until combined.

5. Add the cooked milk mixture to the sugar mixture and stir together.

6. Add the salt, cinnamon, and allspice to the sugar mixture and mix together.

7. Transfer the sugar mixture to a mixing bowl.

8. Sprinkle the instant yeast over the sugar mixture and mix until combined.

9. Slowly add the bread flour to the sugar mixture while mixing and mixing until a dough is formed.

10. Knead the dough until a smooth texture is formed, or for 4-5 minutes.

11. On a floured, plain surface, transfer the dough and shape into a round shape.

12. Grease a bowl lightly and transfer the dough to the greased bowl.

13. Use plastic wrap to cover the dough and set aside for 1-2 hours at room temperature.

14. Drain the soaked fruit and use paper towels to pat it dry.

15. On another floured surface, transfer the dough, knock out the air, and shape into a rectangle.

16. Add the fruit and chopped prunes to the top of the dough.

17. Fold and knead the dough until combined, or for a couple of minutes.

18. Reshape the dough into a rectangle shape and roll into a 9" log.

19. Transfer the dough to a Dutch oven and cover with a lid.

20. Set aside the dough for 45–60 minutes at a warm temperature.

21. Heat up an oven to 375 degrees Fahrenheit.

22. Transfer the Dutch oven, with the lid, to the preheated oven.

23. Bake the dough for 50 minutes.

24. Uncover the Dutch oven and bake the bread for 10 minutes more.

25. Transfer the mixed fruit bread to a cooling rack to cool, slice, and serve.

Nutritional Information/Serving

Calories: 311 kcal, Protein: 6.5g, Fiber: 2.7g, Carbohydrates: 50.9g, Fat: 9.3g

70. Walnut and Fig Bread

Prep Time: 15 minutes

Cook Time: 1 hour, 37 minutes

Serves: 10 servings

Ingredients

For Bread:

2 tbsp. raw sugar

1 ¼ cups of coarsely chopped walnuts

½ cup Greek yogurt

1 tsp. vanilla extract, pure

2 big eggs

¼ cup brown sugar

½ tsp. cardamom

¾ tsp. cinnamon

½ tsp. salt

½ tsp. baking powder

¾ tsp. baking soda

1 cup pastry flour, whole wheat

1 cup of white flour

½ cup plus 2 tbsp. granulated sugar

½ cup plus 2 tbsp. butter

10 figs, halved

For Topping:

Flake sea salt

1 tbsp. fresh rosemary, chopped finely

2 tbsp. honey

½ cup butter, unsalted

Preparation

For Bread:

1. Start by preheating an oven to 350 degrees Fahrenheit.

2. To prepare your Dutch oven, coat the inside with melted butter and a sprinkle of sugar, and set the pot aside.

3. In a skillet over medium heat, combine 2 tablespoons of sugar and 2 tablespoons of butter.

4. Allow the butter to melt, stirring until the sugar blends into it.

5. Add the halved figs to the sugar mixture, placing them cut side down.

6. Saute until the juices thicken and the figs are just caramelized, or for 3-5 minutes.

7. Remove the skillet from the heat and set it aside.

8. Whisk together the cardamom, cinnamon, salt, baking powder, soda, and flours in a big mixing bowl.

9. Moving to your stand mixer with the attached paddle, combine the remaining brown sugar, granulated sugar, and butter.

10. On medium-high speed, mix together for 3 to 5 minutes until the sugars are absorbed by the butter, resulting in a fluffy and light texture (don't forget to pause and give the bowl's sides a gentle scrape with a spatula a couple of times).

11. In a small mixing bowl, mix together the vanilla extract, Greek yogurt, and eggs.

12. Take the mixing bowl off the stand mixer and gracefully fold in the remaining ingredients.

13. In three gentle additions, take turns between the wet and dry ingredients (fold in a third of the dry mixture, followed by half of the wet ingredients, repeating until the cycle concludes with the dry mixture).

14. Incorporate ¾ cup of the walnuts with a final fold.

15. Gently transfer a third of the mixture into your prepared Dutch oven.

16. Lay a delightful stratum of half of the cooked figs on the batter, cover this with another third of the batter, and gracefully place the remaining cooked figs.

17. Top with the final layer of the batter and use a spatula (offset) to smooth the top of the batter for an exquisite finish.

18. Finish off the batter by sprinkling the remaining walnuts and a substantial dusting of raw sugar.

19. Bake the batter for 30 minutes at 350 degrees Fahrenheit, ensuring an even bake by rotating the Dutch oven.

20. Follow the baking process and bake for another 30 minutes in the oven.

21. Reduce the oven temperature to 325 degrees Fahrenheit, rotate the Dutch oven again, and bake until the bred is brown or for an additional 20 to 30 minutes.

22. Leave the bread in the Dutch oven for about 15 to 20 minutes to cool.

23. Transfer the bread to a wire cooling rack to complete the cooling process and slice.

For Topping:

24. Using a stand mixer with the attached whisk, mix together two-thirds of the freshly chopped rosemary, salt, honey, and butter until it becomes fluffy and light.

25. Move the topping to a petite bowl and garnish it with the remaining rosemary and a sprinkle of flake salt.

26. Spread the topping on the sliced walnut and fig bread and serve.

Nutritional Information/Serving

Calories: 492 kcal, Protein: 7.4g, Fiber: 3.3g,
Carbohydrates: 51.4g, Fat: 30.2g

71. Tangerine Basil Bread

Prep Time: 10 minutes

Cook Time: 1 hour

Serves: 10 servings

Ingredients

For Bread:

1/4 cup basil leaves, cut into small pieces

1 lemon, zested

1/2 tbsp. tangerine zest

1 tsp. vanilla extract

1/4 cup lemon-infused olive oil

⅔ cup maple sugar

3/4 cup of fresh tangerine juice

3 medium-size eggs

Salt (pinch)

1 tsp. baking soda

1 bag of Paleo baking flour mix

For Tangerine Glaze:

4 basil leaves, cut into small pieces

1/2 tangerine, zested

2 tbsp. fresh tangerine juice

1/4 cup organic sugar, powdered

For Topping:

Basil leaves

Sliced tangerine

Preparation

For Bread:

1. Heat up an oven to 325° Fahrenheit.

2. Use parchment paper to line a Dutch oven.

3. Add the salt, baking soda, and flour mix to a big bowl and mix together.

4. Add basil leaves, lemon zest, tangerine zest, vanilla, sugar, oil, tangerine juice, and eggs to a medium bowl and mix together.

5. Pour the tangerine juice mixture into the flour mixture and mix until a batter is formed.

6. Transfer the batter to the lined Dutch oven and bake for 55–60 minutes in the preheated oven.

7. Take the Dutch oven from the oven and set it aside for 10 minutes.

8. Transfer the bread to a wire rack to cool.

For Tangerine Glaze:

9. In a bowl, add all the glaze ingredients and mix until combined.

10. Pour the tangerine glaze on top of the bread.

For Topping:

11. Top the tangerine bread with basil leaves and tangerine, and serve.

Nutritional Information/Serving

Calories: 205 kcal, Protein: 4.5g, Fiber: 3.1g, Carbohydrates: 26.6g, Fat: 11.1g

72. Blueberry and Banana Bread

Prep Time: 10 minutes

Cook Time: 1 hour

Serves: 8 servings

Ingredients

1 cup of blueberries

3 medium bananas, ripe and mashed

2 tsp. vanilla extract

2 big eggs

1 cup sugar, granulated

½ cup butter (at room temperature)

½ tsp. salt

½ tsp. baking soda

1 tsp. cinnamon, ground

1 tsp. baking powder

2 cups of white flour

Preparation

1. Heat up an oven to 350° Fahrenheit.

2. Use a nonstick cooking spray to spray a Dutch oven.

3. In a small bowl, add salt, baking soda, cinnamon, baking powder, and white flour, and mix until combined.

4. In a big bowl, add the sugar and butter and mix until fluffy and light.

5. Add the vanilla extract and eggs to the sugar mixture and mix until they combine.

6. Add the banana to the sugar mixture and mix until it combines.

7. Add the flour mixture to the sugar mixture and mix until a batter is formed.

8. Add the blueberries to the batter and lightly mix them together.

9. Add the batter to the sprayed Dutch oven.

10. Bake the batter for 60 minutes in the preheated oven.

11. Take the Dutch oven out of the oven and set it aside for 15 minutes.

12. Transfer the blueberry and banana bread to a wire cooling rack to cool, slice, and serve.

Nutritional Information/Serving

Calories: 384 kcal, Protein: 6g, Fiber: 3g, Carbohydrates: 62g, Fat: 13g

73. Orange Cranberry Bread

Prep Time: 10 minutes

Cook Time: 45 minutes

Serves: 10 servings

Ingredients

¾ cup water, lukewarm

1 cup of orange juice

2 tablespoons of orange zest

1 cup cranberries, dried

⅓ cup pumpkin seeds, unsalted and roasted

1 teaspoon salt

2 tablespoons of vital wheat gluten

¼ teaspoon active dry yeast

½ cup oats, old-fashioned

½ cup whole-wheat flour

2 ½ cups of flour

Preparation

1. In a big mixing bowl, add all the ingredients except water and orange juice.

2. Mix the flour mixture until it combines.

3. Use a spatula to make a well in the middle of the flour mixture.

4. Add the water and orange juice to the well and mix until a dough is formed.

5. Use a towel to cover the dough bowl for 12 to 18 hours at room temperature.

6. Place a lidded Dutch oven in an oven.

7. Heat up the oven to 450° Fahrenheit for 30 minutes.

8. Gently punch down the dough with your fist.

9. Stretch and fold the dough about four times.

10. Use plastic wrap to cover the dough and set aside for 30 minutes.

11. Transfer the dough to the middle of a sheet of parchment paper.

12. Transfer the dough with the parchment paper to the hot Dutch oven and cover with the lid.

13. Bake the dough for 40 minutes in the preheated oven.

14. Uncover the Dutch oven and bake the bread until brown, or for an additional 5 minutes.

15. Transfer the orange cranberry bread to a wire cooling rack to cool, slice, and serve.

Nutritional Information/Serving

Calories: 233 kcal, Protein: 8g, Fiber: 4 g, Carbohydrates: 46g, Fat: 3g

74. Pawpaw Bread

Prep Time: 10 minutes

Cook Time: 1 hour

Serves: 8 servings

Ingredients

3 cups pawpaw pulp

½ tsp. vanilla extract

4 eggs

1 cup of soft butter

2 scant cups of sugar

¼ tsp. salt

2 tsp. baking soda

2½ cups of white flour

Preparation

1. Heat up an oven to 350° Fahrenheit.

2. Use a nonstick cooking spray to spray a Dutch oven.

3. In a bowl, add the salt, baking soda, and white flour and mix together.

4. In another bowl, add butter and sugar and mix until it becomes fluffy and light.

5. Add the vanilla extract and eggs to the sugar mixture and mix together.

6. Add pawpaw pulp to the sugar mixture and mix together.

7. Add the flour mixture to the sugar mixture and mix until a batter is formed.

8. Add the batter to the sprayed Dutch oven.

9. Transfer the Dutch oven to the preheated oven.

10. Bake the batter for 40 minutes to 1 hour.

Nutritional Information/Serving

Calories: 329 kcal, Protein: 9g, Fiber: 1.1g, Carbohydrates: 40.2g, Fat: 15.4g

75. Canary Melon Bread

Prep Time: 5 minutes

Cook Time: 7 minutes

Serves: 8 servings

Ingredients

2 tablespoons of honey

½ cup (chopped) walnuts

½ cup apricot jam

6 ounces of brie cheese, sliced

1 baguette, slice into ½" pieces

1 canary melon, halved and deseeded

Preparation

1. Heat up an oven to 375° Fahrenheit.

2. On each baguette slice, add a teaspoon of apricot jam and spread.

3. Arrange the baguette slices in a Dutch oven.

4. Top the baguette slices with the sliced brie cheese.

5. Bake in the heated oven until the cheese melts, or for 7 minutes.

6. Cut the canary melon into quarters and gently remove the melon rinds.

7. Slice the canary melon.

8. Top the baked bread with the canary melon slices and chopped walnuts.

9. Drizzle the honey over the bread and serve.

Nutritional Information/Serving

Calories: 292 kcal, Protein: 10.4g, Fiber: 14.6g, Carbohydrates: 37.4g, Fat: 11.9g

76. Cranberry No Knead Bread

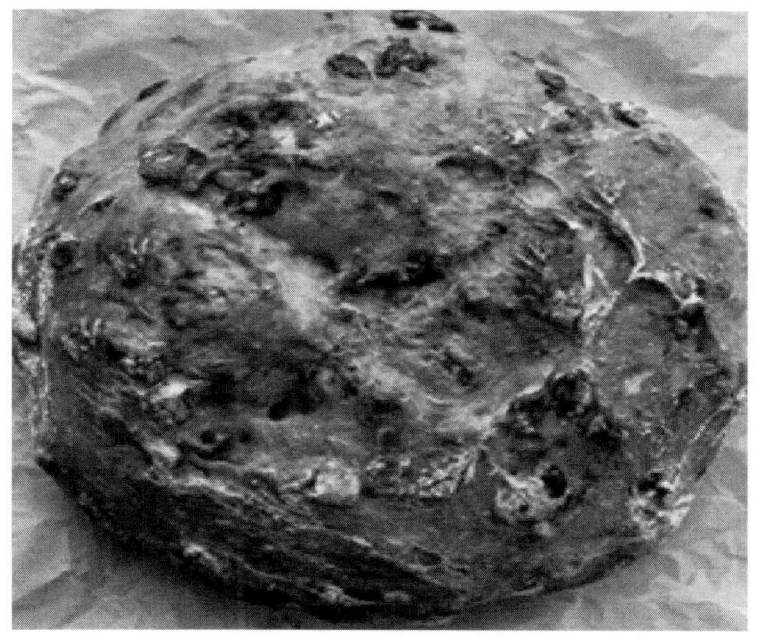

Prep Time: 10 minutes

Cook Time: 45 minutes

Serves: 6 servings

Ingredients

1 1/2 cups of water

1 cup cranberries, dried

1/2 teaspoon instant yeast

1 1/4 teaspoons of salt

3 cups of bread flour

Preparation

1. Add the yeast, salt, and bread flour to a big bowl and mix until combined.

2. Add the water and dried cranberries to the flour mixture and stir until a dough is formed.

3. Shape the dough into a round shape.

4. Cover the dough with cling film and set aside for 18 hours.

5. Transfer the dough to the center of a big sheet of parchment paper.

6. Reshape the dough into a round shape.

7. Transfer the dough with the paper to a Dutch oven with a lid.

8. Cover the Dutch oven with a lid and set aside for 2 hours.

9. Heat up an oven to 450° Fahrenheit.

10. Bake the dough for 30 minutes.

11. Uncover the Dutch oven lid and bake the bread for 15 minutes more.

Nutritional Information/Serving

Calories: 291 kcal, Protein: 8g, Fiber: 3g, Carbohydrates: 62g, Fat: 1g

77. Pineapple Bread

Prep Time: 10 minutes

Cook Time: 1 hour, 5 minutes

Serves: 12 servings

Ingredients

For Bread:

1 teaspoon of vanilla extract

½ cup of sour cream

2 tablespoons of pineapple juice

20 oz. can of crushed pineapple

1 big egg

8 tablespoons of melted, unsalted butter

1 cup of sugar, granulated

Salt (pinch)

½ teaspoon baking powder

1 teaspoon baking soda

2 ¼ cups of white flour

For Pineapple Glaze:

2 tablespoons of pineapple juice

1 cup sugar, powdered

Preparation

For Bread:

1. Heat up an oven to 450° Fahrenheit.

2. Use a nonstick cooking spray to spray a Dutch oven.

3. In a bowl, add the salt, baking powder, soda, and white flour and mix until combined.

4. In a big bowl, add the butter and sugar and mix until fluffy.

5. Add the big egg to the sugar mixture and mix until combined.

6. Add the remaining ingredients to the bowl with the sugar mixture and mix until it combines.

7. Add the flour mixture to the sugar mixture and mix until a batter is formed.

8. Transfer the batter to the sprayed Dutch oven.

9. Bake the batter for 55 minutes to 1 hour and 5 minutes in the heated oven.

10. Let the bread cool in the pan for about 10 minutes.

11. Transfer the bread to a cooling rack to cool.

For Pineapple Glaze:

12. In a bowl, add the glaze ingredients and mix until combined.

13. Pour the pineapple glaze on the pineapple bread, set aside for a few minutes, and slice.

14. Serve the pineapple bread or transfer to a well-lidded container and store for 5 days, or wrap in plastic wrap, transfer to a well-lidded container, and freeze for 3 months.

Nutritional Information/Serving

Calories: 310 kcal, Protein: 3g, Fiber: 1g, Carbohydrates: 53g, Fat: 10g

78. Fig, No-Knead Bread

Prep Time: 10 minutes

Cook Time: 40 minutes

Serves: 12 servings

Ingredients

1 teaspoon of vanilla extract

¼ cup of honey

1½ cups of water, lukewarm

½ cup of roasted walnuts, chopped coarsely

¾ cup (chopped) figs, dried

1 teaspoon salt

1½ teaspoon cinnamon

1 teaspoon of active dry yeast

3½ cups of white flour

Preparation

1. Add the yeast, cinnamon, salt, and white flour to a large ceramic bowl and mix together.

2. Add the chopped walnuts and figs to the flour mixture and stir together.

3. In another bowl, add the remaining ingredients and mix until dissolved.

4. Add the wet mixture to the dry mixture and mix until a dough is formed.

5. Use plastic wrap to tightly cover the dough and set aside for 6–24 hours at room temperature.

6. Transfer the dough to a floured work surface and shape into a round shape (sprinkle flour on the dough if needed).

7. Transfer the shaped dough to the middle of a big sheet of parchment paper.

8. Sprinkle flour on the top of the dough.

9. Use a towel to cover the dough and set aside for 1-2 hours at room temperature.

10. Place a lidded Dutch oven in an oven.

11. Heat up the oven to 450° Fahrenheit for 30 minutes.

12. Use bread lame to score the top of the dough.

13. Transfer the dough with the paper to the heated Dutch oven and cover with a lid.

14. Bake the dough for 30 minutes in the preheated oven.

15. Uncover the Dutch oven lid and bake the bread for an additional 5 to 10 minutes.

16. Transfer the bread to a wire cooling rack to cool, slice, and serve.

Nutritional Information/Serving

Calories: 214 kcal, Protein: 5g, Fiber: 3g, Carbohydrates: 41g, Fat: 4g

79. Lime Bread

Prep Time: 10 minutes

Cook Time: 45 minutes

Serves: 8 servings

Ingredients

For Dough:

1/4 cup of soft butter

2 beaten eggs, divided

2 cups of white flour

1/2 teaspoon salt

1 packet of active dry yeast

2 tablespoons of lime juice

1/4 cup of sugar

1/2 cup milk, warm

For Filling:

2 tablespoons of lime zest

1 cup wild blueberries, dried

1/3 cup of sugar

Preparation

For Dough:

1. In a bowl, add dry yeast, lime juice, 2 tablespoons of sugar, and milk.

2. Mix the milk mixture until it combines, and let stand for 10 minutes.

3. Add the salt and the remaining sugar to the milk mixture and mix together.

4. Add the remaining ingredients to the milk mixture and mix until a dough is formed.

5. Transfer the dough to a sprayed bowl and set aside for 60 minutes at a warm temperature.

For Filling:

6. Add all the filling ingredients to another bowl and mix until combined.

7. Transfer the dough to a floured work surface and shape the dough into a rectangle shape.

8. Add the filling on top of the dough and spread.

9. Reshape the dough into a round shape.

10. Transfer the shaped dough to a sprayed Dutch oven with a lid.

11. Place 15 hot briquettes on the top of the Dutch oven and 7 hot briquettes under the Dutch oven.

12. Bake the dough for 45 minutes (rotate the lid at intervals of 20 minutes).

Nutritional Information/Serving

Calories: 245 kcal, Protein: 5.6g, Fiber: 2g, Carbohydrates: 42.4g, Fat: 5.8g

80. Kiwi Bread

Prep Time: 10 minutes

Cook Time: 50 minutes

Serves: 6 servings

Ingredients

¾ cup pureed kiwi

¼ cup of vanilla almond milk

3 eggs (at room temperature)

½ cup melted butter

½ cup sugar, swerve granular

½ cup of coconut sugar

½ teaspoon of salt

2 teaspoons of baking powder

4 tablespoons of poppy seeds

1 ½ cups of white flour

Preparation

1. Line a Dutch oven with a sheet of parchment paper.

2. Heat up an oven to 350 degrees Fahrenheit.

3. In a bowl, add the sugar and butter, and mix until it is fluffy and light.

4. Add the eggs to the sugar mixture and mix together.

5. Add the salt, poppy seeds, baking powder, and white flour to another bowl and mix until it combines.

6. Gently add the flour mixture to the sugar mixture and mix together.

7. Add the remaining ingredients to the flour mixture and mix until a batter is formed.

8. Transfer the batter to the prepared Dutch oven.

9. Place the Dutch oven on the middle rack of the preheated oven.

10. Bake the batter for 50 minutes.

Nutritional Information/Serving

Calories: 353 kcal, Protein: 4.7g, Fiber: 0.7g, Carbohydrates: 41.6g, Fat: 21.2g

81. Tasty Raspberry Bread

Prep Time: 5 minutes

Cook Time: 30 minutes

Serves: 12 servings

Ingredients

16 ounces of cream cheese frosting

42 ounces of raspberry pie filling

24 doughs, frozen

Preparation

1. Use a sheet of parchment paper to line a 12-inch Dutch oven.

2. Add the frozen dough to the prepared Dutch oven.

3. Add the pie filling over the dough and evenly spread.

4. Transfer the Dutch oven to an oven.

5. Bake the dough for 30 minutes at 350 degrees Fahrenheit.

6. Serve the raspberry bread with the cheese frosting.

Nutritional Information/Serving

Calories: 347 kcal, Protein: 0.5g, Fiber: 4g, Carbohydrates: 38.8g, Fat: 1.4g

82. Crusty Apple Cranberry Bread

Prep Time: 10 minutes

Cook Time: 55 minutes

Serves: 14 servings

Ingredients

1/2 cup of pecans, dried

1/2 cup of cranberries, dried

1 cup of pink apples, diced

1 tsp. cinnamon, ground

1 tbsp. cane sugar

2 tbsp. agave nectar

1 1/2 cups of warm water

3/4 tsp. instant yeast

1 1/4 tsp. salt

2 cups white flour (plus extra for dusting)

2 cups of whole-wheat flour

Preparation

1. Add the yeast, salt, and flour to a big mixing bowl and mix until they combine.

2. In another bowl, add the agave nectar and water and mix until dissolved.

3. Pour the agave nectar mixture into the flour mixture and mix together.

4. Knead the dough for 2 minutes with your hands.

5. Use a silicone cover to cover the dough; set aside for 6–10 hours at a warm temperature.

6. Sprinkle flour on a work surface and transfer the dough to the surface.

7. Punch down the dough and fold it a few times over itself.

8. Spread out the dough to 12-by-10" and sprinkle cinnamon and cane sugar over the top of the dough.

9. Evenly add and spread the pecans, cranberries, and apples to the top of the dough.

10. Tightly shape the dough into a round shape.

11. Transfer the shaped dough to a parchment-lined big bowl.

12. Cover the dough and set aside for 1 to 1 hour, 30 minutes at a warm temperature.

13. Place a lidded Dutch oven in an oven.

14. Heat up the oven to 425 degrees Fahrenheit for 20 minutes.

15. Use bread lame to score the top of the dough.

16. Transfer the dough to the heated Dutch oven, cover with a lid, and bake the dough for 25 minutes.

17. Uncover the Dutch oven and bake the bread for 25–30 minutes more.

Nutritional Information/Serving

Calories: 156 kcal, Protein: 4g, Fiber: 2g, Carbohydrates: 34g, Fat: 0g

83. Red Grape Bread

Prep Time: 10 minutes

Cook Time: 1 hour, 10 minutes

Serves: 12 servings

Ingredients

1 ½ cups of deseeded red grapes, sliced into quarters

½ cup of olive oil

2 tsp. vanilla extract

⅔ cup of milk

2 big eggs (at room temperature)

1 tsp. cinnamon, ground

¼ tsp. salt

1 tbsp. baking powder

1 cup of white sugar, granulated

2 cups of white flour

Preparation

1. Place an oven rack in the middle of an oven.

2. Heat up the oven to 350 degrees Fahrenheit.

3. Use a nonstick cooking spray to spray a Dutch oven.

4. Add the salt, cinnamon, baking powder, sugar, and white flour to a bowl and mix together.

5. Add the olive oil, vanilla extract, milk, and eggs to another bowl and mix together.

6. Pour the olive oil mixture into the flour mixture and mix until a batter is formed.

7. Add the red grape to the batter and lightly mix together.

8. Add the batter to the sprayed Dutch oven.

9. Bake the batter in the heated oven for 1 hour to 1 hour, 10 minutes.

10. Transfer the bread to a wire cooling rack to cool.

11. Serve the red grape bread or tightly wrap it with plastic wrap and store it for 5 days at a warm temperature.

Nutritional Information/Serving

Calories: 257 kcal, Protein: 4g, Fiber: 1g,
Carbohydrates: 37g, Fat: 11g

84. Chocolate Pistachio Bread

Prep Time: 10 minutes

Cook Time: 47 minutes

Serves: 10 servings

Ingredients

For Poolish:

1/2 cup whole-wheat flour

1/2 cup of bread flour

1 pack of dry yeast

1/2 cup water, lukewarm

For Dough:

3/4 cup of white chocolate chips

3/4 cup of cranberries, dried

3/4 cup pistachios

1 teaspoon of orange zest

1 tablespoon of kosher salt

1/2 cup of whole-wheat flour

2 3/4 cups of bread flour

1 cup of water, lukewarm

Preparation

For Poolish:

1. Add a pinch of yeast, water, and flour to a big bowl and mix until combined.

2. Loosely cover the bowl and set it aside for 8 hours at a warm temperature.

For Dough:

3. Add the remaining yeast and lukewarm water to a mixing bowl and mix together.

4. Add the poolish to the yeast mixture and stir together.

5. Add the orange zest, salt, and flour to the poolish mixture and mix for 4 minutes on low speed.

6. Use a cooking spray to lightly grease a big bowl.

7. Transfer the dough to the greased bowl, cover, and let stand for 30 minutes.

8. Stretch and fold the dough over itself four times.

9. Evenly add the remaining ingredients to the dough.

10. Cover the dough and let it stand for 30 minutes at room temperature.

11. Fold the dough again, cover, and set aside for 30 minutes.

12. Use parchment paper to line a banneton.

13. Transfer the dough to a floured work surface and shape the dough into a 1"-thick disk.

14. Stretch and fold the dough again and shape it into a round shape.

15. Transfer the shaped dough to the lined banana, cover, and set aside for 45–60 minutes at room temperature.

16. Place a lidded Dutch oven in an oven.

17. Heat up the oven to 450° Fahrenheit for 20 minutes.

18. Use bread lame to score the top of the dough and transfer it to the hot Dutch oven.

19. Cover the Dutch oven with a lid and bake the dough for 40 minutes at 400° Fahrenheit.

20. Uncover the Dutch oven and bake the bread for an additional 5 to 7 minutes.

21. Transfer the chocolate pistachio bread to a cooling rack to cool, slice, and serve.

Nutritional Information/Serving

Calories: 353 kcal, Protein: 7.8g, Fiber: 3.7g, Carbohydrates: 62.6g, Fat: 7.8g

85. Date and Walnut Bread

Prep Time: 10 minutes

Cook Time: 1 hour

Serves: 8 servings

Ingredients

1 1/2 cups of water, cool

1/2 cup of dates, chopped

1 cup of walnuts, chopped

1 teaspoon salt

1/2 teaspoon yeast

1 1/2 cups white flour, unbleached

1 1/2 cups of whole-wheat flour

Preparation

1. In a bowl, add the dates, walnuts, salt, yeast, and flour and mix together.

2. Add water to the flour mixture and mix until a dough is formed.

3. Use a kitchen towel to cover the dough and set aside for 18–24 hours at room temperature.

4. Shape the dough into a round shape.

5. Transfer the shaped dough to a generously floured kitchen towel.

6. Wrap the floured towel over the shaped dough and set aside for 1 hour, 30 minutes, or 2 hours.

7. Place a lidded Dutch oven in an oven.

8. Heat up the oven to 475°F for 30 minutes.

9. Gently transfer the dough to the heated Dutch oven with the seam side facing up.

10. Cover the Dutch oven with a lid, and bake the dough for 30 minutes.

11. Uncover the Dutch oven lid and bake the bread for 15 to 30 minutes more.

Nutritional Information/Serving

Calories: 279 kcal, Protein: 8g, Fiber: 5.1g, Carbohydrates: 39.6g, Fat: 10.2g

86. Nut and Fruit Bread

Prep Time: 10 minutes

Cook Time: 45 minutes

Serves: 10 servings

Ingredients

1 ½ cups of water

½ cup of pecans

½ cup of walnuts

½ cup of golden raisins

½ cup of cranberries, dried

2 tsp. of salt

¾ tsp. of instant yeast

1 cup of whole-wheat flour

3 cups of white flour

Preparation

1. In a big bowl, add the yeast, salt, and flours and mix until combined.

2. Add the nuts and fruit to the flour mixture and stir together.

3. Add the water to the flour mixture and mix until a dough is formed.

4. Cover the dough bowl and set aside for 12–18 hours at a warm temperature.

5. On a work surface, lay a sheet of parchment paper and dust with flour.

6. Transfer the dough to the prepared paper and fold it a few times over itself.

7. Shape the dough into a ball shape and place it on the parchment paper with the seam side facing down.

8. Sprinkle flour over the shaped dough, cover, and set aside for 2 hours.

9. Place a Dutch oven with a lid in the oven.

10. For 30 minutes, heat up the oven to 425 degrees Fahrenheit.

11. Use a bread lame to score the top of the dough with 3 slashes.

12. Transfer the dough to the heated Dutch oven with the parchment paper.

13. Cover the Dutch oven with a lid, and bake the dough for 30 minutes.

14. Uncover the Dutch oven and bake the bread for 10–15 minutes more.

15. Transfer the bread to a wire cooling rack to cool and serve.

Nutritional Information/Serving

Calories: 306 kcal, Protein: 7.1g, Fiber: 4.4g, Carbohydrates: 51.4g, Fat: 8g

87. Easy Orange Bread

Prep Time: 10 minutes

Cook Time: 40 minutes

Serves: 10 servings

Ingredients

2 tbsp. olive oil

3/4 cup of orange juice

1 egg

1 orange, zested

1 cup of cranberries, fresh

1/2 cup of slivered almonds

1/2 tsp. of baking soda

1 tsp. of salt

1/2 tbsp. of baking powder

3/4 cup of sugar

2 cups of white flour

Preparation

1. Heat up an oven to 350 degrees Fahrenheit.

2. In a big bowl, add the salt, baking powder, baking soda, sugar, and white flour and mix together.

3. In a medium bowl, add the olive oil, orange zest, orange juice, and egg, and mix until combined.

4. Add the flour mixture to the orange mixture and mix until a batter is formed.

5. Fold in the almonds and fresh cranberries to the batter and lightly mix together.

6. Add the batter to a greased Dutch oven.

7. Place the Dutch oven in the heated oven and bake for 40 minutes.

Nutritional Information/Serving

Calories: 247 kcal, Protein: 5g, Fiber: 3g,
Carbohydrates: 44g, Fat: 6g

88. Rosemary Lime Bread

Prep Time: 10 minutes

Cook Time: 1 hour

Serves: 10 servings

Ingredients

1 ⅓ cups of water, lukewarm

2 tsp. lime zest

2 tsp. rosemary, freshly chopped

1 ½ tsp. kosher salt

¼ tsp. active dry yeast

3 cups flour (plus more for sprinkling)

Preparation

1. In a bowl, add all the ingredients except water, and mix until combined.

2. Add water to the flour mixture and mix until a dough is formed.

3. Use a nonstick cooking spray to spray a bowl.

4. Transfer the dough to the sprayed bowl, cover, and set aside for 12 to 18 hours at a warm temperature.

5. Lightly sprinkle flour on a work surface and transfer the dough to the surface.

6. Sprinkle flour over the dough and knead lightly for 1 minute.

7. Use plastic wrap to cover the dough and set aside for 15 minutes.

8. Coat a kitchen towel with flour.

9. Shape the dough into a round shape.

10. Transfer the dough to the middle of the floured kitchen towel with the seam side facing down.

11. Use flour to dust the top of the shaped dough and loosely wrap the dough with the towel.

12. Transfer the wrapped dough to a big bowl and set aside for 1 hour, 30 minutes, or 2 hours.

13. Place a lidded Dutch oven in an oven.

14. Heat up the oven to 450 degrees Fahrenheit for 30 minutes.

15. Transfer the dough to the hot Dutch oven and cover with a lid.

16. Bake the dough for 30 minutes.

17. Remove the Dutch oven lid and bake the bread until brown, or for 15 to 30 minutes more.

18. Transfer the bread to a cooling rack to cool, slice, and serve.

Nutritional Information/Serving

Calories: 137 kcal, Protein: 3.9g, Fiber: 1.1g, Carbohydrates: 28.8g, Fat: 0.4g

89. Cherry and Chocolate Bread

Prep Time: 10 minutes

Cook Time: 50 minutes

Serves: 12 servings

Ingredients

1 ¼ cups of toasted and chopped walnuts

½ cup of chocolate chips, semi-sweet

¾ cup of cherries, dried

1 ⅔ cups water, cool

2 tbsp. sugar

¼ cup of cocoa powder, Dutch-processed

2 tsp. salt

1 tsp. active dry yeast

1 cup of medium rye flour

3 cups of unbleached flour

Preparation

1. In a big bowl, add the sugar, cocoa powder, salt, yeast, and flours, and mix together.

2. Add the cool water to the flour mixture and mix until a dough is formed.

3. Add the remaining ingredients to the dough and lightly mix them together.

4. Use plastic wrap to cover the dough and set aside for 12 to 18 hours at a warm temperature.

5. On a floured work surface, transfer the dough and lightly dust the top with flour.

6. Knead the dough lightly for 1 minute.

7. Use plastic wrap to cover the dough and set aside for 15 minutes.

8. Use flour to coat a cotton towel.

9. Shape the dough into a round shape.

10. Transfer the dough to the middle of the prepared cotton towel with the seam side facing down.

11. Lightly sprinkle flour over the dough and wrap the dough loosely with the towel.

12. In a big bowl, transfer the dough with the towel and set aside for 1 hour, 30 minutes to 2 hours.

13. Place a lidded Dutch oven in an oven.

14. Heat up the oven to 450 degrees Fahrenheit for 30 minutes.

15. Transfer the dough to the heated Dutch oven with the seam side facing up.

16. Place a lid on the Dutch oven and bake the dough for 20 minutes.

17. Uncover the Dutch oven and bake the bread for 20 to 30 minutes more.

18. Transfer the cherries and chocolate bread to a wire cooling rack to cool.

19. Serve the bread, or tightly wrap and freeze for 12 weeks or on a counter for 5 days.

Nutritional Information/Serving

Calories: 306 kcal, Protein: 8.7g, Fiber: 5g, Carbohydrates: 46g, Fat: 10.6g

90. Mango Bread

Prep Time: 10 minutes

Cook Time: 1 hour, 30 minutes

Serves: 24 servings

Ingredients

1 cup of raisins

1 cup of walnuts, chopped

4 cups of peeled and chopped mangoes

2 tsp. vanilla extract

1 1/2 cups of olive oil

6 big eggs

1 tsp. salt

3 tsp. baking soda

4 tsp. of cinnamon, ground

2 1/2 cups of sugar

4 cups of white flour

Preparation

1. Heat up an oven to 325 degrees Fahrenheit.

2. Add the salt, baking soda, cinnamon, sugar, and white flour to a big bowl and mix together.

3. Add vanilla extract, olive oil, and eggs to another bowl and mix until they combine.

4. Add the oil mixture to the flour mixture and mix until combined.

5. Add the remaining ingredients to the flour mixture and mix together.

6. Transfer the flour mixture to a Dutch oven lined with a sheet of parchment paper.

7. Place the Dutch oven in the preheated oven and bake for 1 hour, 15 minutes to 1 hour, 30 minutes.

8. Transfer the mango bread to a cooling rack to cool, slice, and serve.

Nutritional Information/Serving

Calories: 317 kcal, Protein: 4g, Fiber: 1g, Carbohydrates: 42g, Fat: 16g

91. Blueberry and Lime Bread

Prep Time: 10 minutes

Cook Time: 40 minutes

Serves: 16 servings

Ingredients

Salt (a pinch)

2 cups water, warm

2 tbsp. olive oil

1 pack of yeast, rapid rise

4 cups of white flour

¼ cup of soft butter, unsalted

½ cup of brown sugar.

1 tbsp. lime juice

1 cup of blueberries

Preparation

1. Add the water and yeast to a mixing bowl and mix until combined.

2. Set aside the yeast mixture for 10 minutes.

3. Add the salt and white flour to a second bowl and stir together.

4. Add 1/4 cup of sugar to the flour mixture and mix together.

5. Pour the yeast mixture into the flour mixture and mix until a dough is formed.

6. Drizzle the oil over the dough, cover, and set aside for 60 minutes.

7. Add the remaining ingredients to a small bowl and mix together.

8. Add the blueberry mixture to the dough and mix together.

9. Cover the dough and set it aside for 30 minutes.

10. Grease a Dutch oven with oil.

11. Place the greased Dutch oven in an oven.

12. Heat up the oven to 400°F for 30 minutes.

13. Transfer the dough to the hot Dutch oven and cover with a lid.

14. Bake the dough for 30 minutes.

15. Remove the Dutch oven lid and bake the bread for 10 minutes more.

16. Transfer the bread to a cooling rack to cool, slice, and serve.

Nutritional Information/Serving

Calories: 183 kcal, Protein: 4g, Fiber: 1g, Carbohydrates: 31g, Fat: 5g

92. Cardamom Honey Bread

Prep Time: 10 minutes

Cook Time: 45 minutes

Serves: 8 servings

Ingredients

For Bread:

2 tbsp. honey

1 tsp. cardamom, ground

2 1/2 tsp. orange zest, grated finely

1 1/3 cups of water

1/4 tsp. of active dry yeast

1/2 tsp. of salt

3 cups of bread flour (plus more for dusting)

For Butter Topping:

1 tsp. of maple syrup

2 tsp. of dark brown sugar

1 tsp. cardamom, ground

2 tsp. of peeled ginger, grated finely

1 tsp. of fresh orange juice

2 tsp. orange zest, grated finely

1/2 cup of butter, unsalted and softened

Preparation

For Bread:

1. Add all the bread ingredients except water to a big bowl and mix until combined.

2. Add the water to the flour mixture and mix until a dough is formed.

3. Use plastic wrap to cover the dough bowl and set aside for 12 to 18 hours at room temperature.

4. Use flour to dust a work surface and a cotton towel generously.

5. Transfer the dough to the floured work surface and shape the dough into a round shape.

6. Transfer the shaped dough to the prepared towel with the seam side facing down.

7. Sprinkle flour over the dough and wrap the towel over the dough.

8. Set aside the dough for 2 hours.

9. Place a lidded Dutch oven in an oven and heat up the oven to 450 degrees Fahrenheit for 30 minutes.

10. Transfer the dough to the hot Dutch oven and cover with a lid.

11. Bake the dough for 30 minutes.

12. Remove the Dutch oven lid and bake the bread until golden, or for 15 minutes more.

13. Transfer the bread to a cooling rack to cool and slice.

For Butter Topping:

14. Add all the butter topping ingredients to a bowl and mix until they combine.

15. Top the sliced cardamom honey bread with the butter topping and serve.

Nutritional Information/Serving

Calories: 313 kcal, Protein: 6.4g, Fiber: 1.5g, Carbohydrates: 44.1g, Fat: 12.4g

93. Tasty Pear Bread

Prep Time: 10 minutes

Cook Time: 1 hour

Serves: 32 servings

Ingredients

1 cup of chopped pecans

1 tsp. salt

1 tsp. baking soda

2 tsp. cinnamon

2 tsp. baking powder

3 cups of flour

1 tsp. vanilla extract

½ cup of brown sugar

¾ cup of olive oil

1 cup of sugar, granulated

3 eggs (at room temperature)

1 tsp. lime juice

4 cups of ripe pears, peeled and chopped finely

Preparation

1. Grease a Dutch oven with butter and heat up the oven to 350 degrees Fahrenheit.

2. In a bowl, add the lime juice and pears and stir together.

3. Add vanilla extract, brown sugar, olive oil, sugar, and eggs to a big bowl and mix until they combine.

4. Add the remaining ingredients to a third bowl and stir together.

5. Add the egg mixture to the flour mixture and mix until a batter is formed.

6. Add the pear mixture to the batter and mix until it combines.

7. Transfer the batter to the prepared Dutch oven.

8. Bake the batter for 55 minutes to 1 hour in the preheated oven.

9. Transfer the bread to a cooling rack to cool.

10. Serve the pear bread or transfer it to a well-lidded container and refrigerate.

Nutritional Information/Serving

Calories: 166 kcal, Protein: 2g, Fiber: 1g, Carbohydrates: 22g, Fat: 8g

94. Banana and Butter Bread

Prep Time: 10 minutes

Cook Time: 30 minutes

Serves: 8 servings

Ingredients

1 (beaten) egg

½ cup of soft butter

4 ripe bananas, mashed

Salt (pinch)

1 tsp. of baking soda

2 tsp. of cinnamon

1 cup of brown sugar

1 ½ cups of white flour

Preparation

1. In a bowl, add the salt, baking soda, cinnamon, sugar, and white flour and mix together.

2. Heat up a 20-coal campfire.

3. Add the egg, butter, and banana to another bowl and mix until they combine.

4. Add the flour mixture to the banana mixture and mix until a batter is formed.

5. Use a piece of parchment paper to line a Dutch oven.

6. Transfer the batter to the lined Dutch oven and cover with a lid.

7. Place the hot 5 coal rings at the bottom of the Dutch oven and the 15 coal rings on top of the Dutch oven lid.

8. Bake the batter for 30 minutes.

9. Transfer the banana and butter bread to a cooling rack to cool, slice, and serve.

Nutritional Information/Serving

Calories: 353 kcal, Protein: 4.5g, Carbohydrates: 62.5g, Fat: 12.5g

95. Honey Lemon Bread

Prep Time: 10 minutes

Cook Time: 45 minutes

Serves: 8 servings

Ingredients

1/2 teaspoon of lemon

1 teaspoon of kosher salt

1 tablespoon of honey

1 1/2 teaspoons of yeast

375 g of water (at room temperature)

500 g of white flour

Preparation

1. In a mixing bowl, add 100g of water and 125g of white flour and mix until combined.

2. Set aside the flour mixture for 15 minutes.

3. Add the remaining ingredients to the flour mixture and mix for 5 minutes or until a dough is formed.

4. Use plastic wrap to cover the dough bowl and set aside for 20 minutes.

5. Stretch and fold the dough over itself and shape it into a round shape.

6. Cover the dough again, and set it aside for 60 minutes.

7. Lightly sprinkle flour on a work surface and transfer the dough to the surface.

8. Reshape the dough into a tight, round shape.

9. Use flour to dust a banneton.

10. Transfer the shaped dough to the banneton with the seam side facing down.

11. Use plastic wrap to cover the banneton and set aside for 60 minutes.

12. Place a lidded Dutch oven on the center rack of an oven.

13. Heat up the oven to 475 degrees Fahrenheit for 20 minutes.

14. Transfer the dough to the middle of a piece of parchment paper.

15. Use bread lame to score the top of the dough.

16. Transfer the dough with the parchment paper to the hot Dutch oven and cover with a lid.

17. Bake the dough in the preheated oven for 35 minutes.

18. Remove the Dutch oven lid and bake the bread for 10 minutes more.

Nutritional Information/Serving

Calories: 240 kcal, Protein: 7g, Fiber: 1.9g, Carbohydrates: 50.6g, Fat: 0.6g

96. Red Apple Bread

Prep Time: 10 minutes

Cook Time: 40 minutes

Serves: 10 servings

Ingredients

2 big peeled red apples, sliced into bite-size

Salt (a pinch)

25 g of sugar

20 ml of milk

480 ml of cool water

1020 g of white flour, unbleached (plus more for dusting)

14 g of active dry yeast

220 ml of warm water

Preparation

1. Add the 7 g of yeast and warm water to a bowl and stir together.

2. Set aside the yeast mixture for 8 to 10 minutes.

3. Add 220g of white flour to the yeast mixture and mix until combined.

4. Use a kitchen towel to cover the flour mixture and set it aside for 12 hours at a warm temperature.

5. Add the remaining ingredients, except the apples, to the flour mixture and mix until a dough forms.

6. Knead the dough for 20 minutes on low speed.

7. Use a tea towel to cover the dough bowl and set it aside at a warm temperature for 45 minutes.

8. Add the apples to the dough and lightly fold.

9. Line a bowl with parchment paper.

10. Transfer the dough to the prepared bowl, cover, and set aside at a warm temperature for 45 minutes.

11. Place a lidded Dutch oven in an oven.

12. Heat up the oven to 450 degrees Fahrenheit for 30 minutes.

13. Transfer the dough with the parchment paper to the hot Dutch oven and cover with the lid.

14. Bake the dough for 30 minutes.

15. Remove the Dutch oven lid and bake the bread for 10 minutes more.

Nutritional Information/Serving

Calories: 399 kcal, Protein: 14g, Fiber: 5g,
Carbohydrates: 81g, Fat: 0.1g

Chapter 9: Cheese Breads

97. Jalapeno and Cheddar Bread

Prep Time: 15 minutes

Cook Time: 50 minutes

Serves: 8 servings

Ingredients

1 (sliced) jalapeño

1 big (whisked) egg

2¼ tsp. instant yeast

2 cups of warm water

1 tablespoon of water

2 tsp. paprika, smoked

1 tsp. black pepper, ground

1 tbsp. salt

4 slices of cooked bacon, chopped

2 deseeded jalapeños, chopped

3 cups of cheddar cheese, shredded

3½ cups of bread flour

Preparation

1. In a big bowl, add the paprika, pepper, salt, bacon, jalapenos, 2 cups of cheese, and bread flour.

2. Mix the flour mixture until combined.

3. Add instant yeast and water to another bowl and mix together.

4. Add the yeast mixture to the flour mixture and mix until a dough is formed.

5. Stretch and fold the dough a few times over itself.

6. Cover the dough with a tea towel and set it aside for 60 minutes.

7. Stretch and fold the dough again a few times over itself, cover, and set aside for 30 minutes.

8. Place a lidded Dutch oven in an oven.

9. Heat up the oven to 450 degrees Fahrenheit for 30 minutes.

10. Lightly sprinkle flour on a work surface.

11. Transfer the dough to the floured surface.

12. Fold the dough and transfer it to the middle of a piece of parchment paper.

13. In a small bowl, add a tablespoon of water and an egg, and stir together.

14. Use the egg mixture to gently brush the dough.

15. Add the jalapenos slices and the remaining shredded cheese to the dough.

16. Use bread lame to score the top of the dough.

17. Transfer the dough to the hot Dutch oven with the parchment paper.

18. Cover the Dutch oven with a lid and bake the dough for 30 minutes.

19. Remove the Dutch oven lid and bake the bread for 20 minutes more.

20. Transfer the bread to a cooling rack to cool.

21. Serve bread or transfer to a well-lidded container, freeze for 3 months, or refrigerate for 7 days.

Nutritional Information/Serving

Calories: 343 kcal, Protein: 14.2g, Fiber: 3.2g, Carbohydrates: 51.7g, Fat: 8.9g

98. Parmesan Rosemary Bread

Prep Time: 10 minutes

Cook Time: 50 minutes

Serves: 6 servings

Ingredients

½ tbsp. olive oil

1 cup shredded Parmesan cheese

1 ½ tbsp. rosemary, dried

1 ¾ cups of water, warm

2 teaspoons of salt

3 ¼ cups of white flour

¼ tsp. of instant yeast

Preparation

1. In a big bowl, add the dried rosemary, salt, yeast, and white flour, and mix until combined.

2. Add water to the flour mixture and mix until a dough is formed.

3. Use a kitchen towel to cover the dough and set it aside for 12 to 18 hours.

4. Lightly sprinkle flour on a piece of parchment paper.

5. Shape the dough into a round shape and transfer it to the prepared parchment paper.

6. Sprinkle flour over the dough, cover loosely with a kitchen towel, and set aside.

7. Place a lidded Dutch oven in an oven.

8. Heat up the oven to 450° Fahrenheit.

9. Drizzle the oil over the dough.

10. Evenly sprinkle the dried rosemary and cheese over the top of the dough.

11. Transfer the dough with the parchment paper to the hot Dutch oven and cover with a lid.

12. Bake the dough for 30 minutes.

13. Remove the Dutch oven lid and bake the bread until brown, or for an additional 10 to 20 minutes.

Nutritional Information/Serving

Calories: 336 kcal, Protein: 14g, Fiber: 3g, Carbohydrates: 55g, Fat: 6g

99. Gruyere Cheese Bread

Prep Time: 10 minutes

Cook Time: 45 minutes

Serves: 12 servings

Ingredients

3 cups of bread flour

2 teaspoons of instant yeast

1 1/2 teaspoons of kosher salt

1 1/2 cups of warm water

2 1/2 cups of fresh Gruyere cheese, shredded

Preparation

1. In a big bowl, add the yeast, salt, and bread flour and stir together.

2. Add warm water to the flour mixture and mix until a dough is formed.

3. Use cling wrap to cover the dough and set aside for 2-3 hours at room temperature.

4. Place a lidded Dutch oven in an oven.

5. Heat up the oven to 450 degrees Fahrenheit for 30 minutes.

6. Transfer the dough to a lightly floured work surface.

7. Shape the dough into a round shape.

8. Evenly add and spread the shredded cheese over the dough.

9. Fold the dough, reshape it into a round shape, and transfer it to the middle of a piece of parchment paper.

10. Transfer the dough with the parchment paper to the hot Dutch oven.

11. Cover the Dutch oven with a lid, and bake the dough for 35 minutes.

12. Remove the Dutch oven lid and bake the bread for 10 minutes more.

13. Transfer the bread to a wire rack to cool.

Nutritional Information/Serving

Calories: 273 kcal, Protein: 13g, Fiber: 2g,
Carbohydrates: 29g, Fat: 11g

100. Cheddar and Olive Bread

Prep Time: 10 minutes

Cook Time: 40 minutes

Serves: 8 servings

Ingredients

3/4 cup of green olives, sliced

2 1/2 cups of extra-sharp cheddar, shredded

1 tbsp. olive oil

3/4 cup of milk

1 tsp. black pepper

1/2 tsp. salt

3 1/2 cups of bread flour

1 tsp. sugar

1 pack of yeast

1/2 cup of water, lukewarm

Preparation

1. In a bowl, add sugar, yeast, and water, stir together, and set aside.

2. Add pepper, salt, and flour to a big bowl and mix together.

3. Add the sliced olives, shredded cheese, and yeast mixture to the flour mixture and lightly mix together.

4. Add the oil and milk to the flour mixture and mix until a dough is formed.

5. Sprinkle flour on a pastry cloth, transfer the dough, and knead until a smooth texture is formed.

6. Transfer the dough to a greased bowl, cover, and set aside for 1-4 hours at room temperature.

7. Shape the dough into a round shape and transfer it to a Dutch oven.

8. Cover the Dutch oven with a damp kitchen towel and set aside for 1-2 hours.

9. Heat up the oven to 350 degrees Fahrenheit.

10. Transfer the Dutch oven to the preheated oven and bake for 35–40 minutes.

Nutritional Information/Serving

Calories: 311 kcal, Protein: 11.2g, Fiber: 2.3g, Carbohydrates: 47.4g, Fat: 8.5g

101. Garlic and Mozzarella Bread

Prep Time: 10 minutes

Cook Time: 15 minutes

Serves: 4 servings

Ingredients

1/4 cup of freshly chopped basil

1/4 teaspoon of salt

1/2 cup of soft butter, unsalted

3 big garlic cloves, minced

6 ounces of mozzarella cheese, shredded

1 round of sourdough bread, sliced horizontally

Preparation

1. In a bowl, add butter, salt, and garlic and mix until combined.

2. Heat 22 to 25 briquettes in a charcoal chimney.

3. Add the butter mixture to one side of each sliced sourdough bread and spread.

4. Evenly divide the cheese among the bread slices.

5. Vertically slice the bread slices to make a small square shape.

6. Use a piece of parchment paper to line a Dutch oven.

7. Transfer the bread slices to the lined Dutch oven.

8. Cover the Dutch oven with a lid.

9. Place the hot on the bottom and top of the Dutch oven (to make 425 degrees Fahrenheit).

10. Bake the bread until the cheese melts, or for 15 minutes.

11. Top the bread with fresh basil and serve.

Nutritional Information/Serving

Calories: 289 kcal, Protein: 14.6g, Fiber: 2g, Carbohydrates: 9.2g, Fat: 23.3g

102. Italian Cheese Bread

Prep Time: 5 minutes

Cook Time: 45 minutes

Serves: 8 servings

Ingredients

1/2 cup of mozzarella cheese, shredded

3/4 tsp. Italian seasoning

1 1/2 cups of water, warm

1/2 tsp. of active dry yeast

1 3/4 tsp. of salt

4 cups of white flour

Preparation

1. Add water, yeast, salt, and white flour to a large bowl and mix until combined.

2. Use plastic wrap to cover the flour mixture and set aside for 8 hours.

3. Place a lidded Dutch oven in an oven and heat up the oven to 450° Fahrenheit.

4. Sprinkle flour on a work surface and transfer the dough to the surface.

5. Add the shredded cheese and 1/2 teaspoon of seasoning to the dough.

6. Knead the dough and shape it into a round shape.

7. Transfer the shaped dough to a greased Dutch oven.

8. Sprinkle the remaining seasoning over the dough.

9. Cover the Dutch oven with a lid.

10. Bake the dough for 30 minutes.

11. Remove the Dutch oven lid and bake until the bread is brown, or for 15 minutes more.

Nutritional Information/Serving

Calories: 248 kcal, Protein: 8.2g, Fiber: 1.8g, Carbohydrates: 48g, Fat: 2.1g

103. Cheese and Herb Bread

Prep Time: 10 minutes

Cook Time: 50 minutes

Serves: 10 servings

Ingredients

1 ⅔ cups of water, warm

½ teaspoon powdered garlic

1¼ teaspoons of salt

3 fresh rosemary stalks, chopped finely

4 fresh thyme stalks, de-stemmed

¾ cup grated Gruyere cheese

1 teaspoon of instant yeast

3 cups of flour (plus extra for sprinkling)

Preparation

1. In a big mixing bowl, add the instant yeast and flour, and mix together.

2. Add the remaining ingredients, except water, to the flour mixture and mix together.

3. Add the warm water to the flour mixture and mix until a dough is formed.

4. Cover the dough bowl and set it aside for 16 hours at room temperature.

5. Lightly sprinkle flour on a work surface.

6. Transfer the dough to the prepared surface.

7. Fold the dough and shape it into a round shape.

8. Transfer the shaped dough to a floured bowl, cover, and set aside for 60 minutes.

9. Place a lidded Dutch oven in an oven.

10. For 30 minutes, heat up the oven to 400 degrees Fahrenheit.

11. Transfer the dough to the center of a big piece of parchment paper.

12. Transfer the dough with the parchment paper to the hot Dutch oven.

13. Place a lid on the Dutch oven and bake the dough for 30 minutes.

14. Remove the Dutch oven lid and bake the bread until brown, or for 20 minutes more.

Nutritional Information/Serving

Calories: 183 kcal, Protein: 7g, Fiber: 1g, Carbohydrates: 29g, Fat: 4g

104. Sage Cheese Bread

Prep Time: 10 minutes

Cook Time: 40 minutes

Serves: 8 servings

Ingredients

Corn flour (for sprinkling)

1 tsp. of rubbed sage

4 oz. block of white cheddar cheese, grated

4 oz. block of white cheddar cheese, cubed

1 ¾ cups + 2 tbsp. warm water

2¼ tsp. instant yeast

1 tbsp. kosher salt

1 cup of whole-wheat flour

3 cups of bread flour

Preparation

1. Add the instant yeast, salt, and flour to a big bowl and mix together.

2. Add water to the flour mixture and mix until a dough is formed.

3. Cover the dough bowl and set it aside for 2 hours at room temperature.

4. Add sage and grated cheese to a small bowl and mix together.

5. On a floured work surface, transfer the dough and lightly sprinkle four over the dough.

6. Roll the dough into a thickness of 1".

7. Sprinkle the cheese mixture and cubed cheddar cheese over the dough.

8. Fold the dough and reroll into a thickness of 1".

9. Shape the dough into a tight round shape.

10. Sprinkle corn flour on a piece of parchment paper.

11. Transfer the dough to the floured parchment paper with the seam side facing up.

12. Cover the dough and set it aside for 60 minutes at room temperature.

13. Place a lidded Dutch oven in an oven.

14. Heat up the oven to 500 degrees Fahrenheit for 30 minutes.

15. Transfer the dough to the hot Dutch oven.

16. Use bread lame to score the dough.

17. Place a lid on the Dutch oven and bake the dough for 25 minutes at 450 degrees Fahrenheit.

18. Remove the Dutch oven lid and bake the bread for an additional 15 minutes.

Nutritional Information/Serving

Calories: 360 kcal, Protein: 15.6g, Fiber: 3.6g, Carbohydrates: 50.9g, Fat: 10.2g

105. Cheese and Ham Bread

Prep Time: 10 minutes

Cook Time: 45 minutes

Serves: 12 servings

Ingredients

2 cups of ham, cooked and diced

2 cups grated sharp cheddar cheese

Cornmeal

2 teaspoons of yeast

3 tsp. kosher salt

3 cups of water, lukewarm

6 cups of white flour (plus extra for dusting)

Preparation

1. Add yeast, salt, and white flour to a big bowl and mix together.

2. Add lukewarm water to the flour mixture and mix until a dough is formed.

3. Use plastic wrap to cover the dough and set aside for 8 to 18 hours at a warm temperature.

4. Add the grated cheese and ham to the dough and mix together.

5. Transfer the dough to a floured work surface and shape into a round shape.

6. Transfer the shaped dough to a greased bowl, cover, and set aside for 60 minutes.

7. Use a cooking spray to spray a pan.

8. Sprinkle the cornmeal on the sprayed pan.

9. Place a lidded Dutch oven in an oven.

10. Heat up the oven to 450 degrees Fahrenheit for 30 minutes.

11. Transfer the dough to the hot Dutch oven and cover with a lid.

12. Bake the dough for 30 minutes.

13. Remove the Dutch oven lid and bake the bread for 15 minutes more.

14. Transfer the bread to a cooling rack to cool, slice, and serve.

Nutritional Information/Serving

Calories: 156 kcal, Protein: 11.6g, Fiber: 0.2g, Carbohydrates: 5.1g, Fat: 9.9g

Chapter 10: Nut, Seed, and Grain Breads

106. Flaxseed Yogurt Bread

Prep Time: 10 minutes

Cook Time: 40 minutes

Serves: 6 servings

Ingredients

½ cup of low-fat yogurt

¾ cup of water, lukewarm

1 tsp. honey

1 pack of dry yeast

3 tbsp. of flaxseed

2 tsp. salt

1 cup of whole-wheat flour

2 1/2 cups of white flour

Preparation

1. In a mixing bowl, add the flaxseed, salt, and flour, and mix together.

2. In a small bowl, add water, honey, and yeast and mix until combined.

3. Set aside the yeast mixture for 5 minutes.

4. Add yogurt to the yeast mixture and stir together.

5. Pour the yeast mixture into the flour mixture and mix until a dough is formed.

6. Lightly sprinkle flour on a work surface.

7. Transfer the dough to the prepared surface, knead, and shape the dough into a ball shape.

8. Transfer the shaped dough to a floured bowl, cover, and set aside for 60 minutes at a warm temperature.

9. Return the dough to the floured work surface and knead.

10. Reshape the dough and transfer it to the middle of a sheet of parchment paper.

11. Use a kitchen towel to cover the dough and set it aside for 60 minutes.

12. Place a lidded Dutch oven in an oven.

13. Heat up the oven to 450 degrees Fahrenheit for 30 minutes.

14. Transfer the dough to the hot Dutch oven with the parchment paper and cover with a lid.

15. Bake the dough for 25 minutes.

16. Remove the Dutch oven lid and bake the bread until brown, or for 10 to 15 minutes more.

17. Transfer the bread to a cooling rack to cool, slice, and serve.

Nutritional Information/Serving

Calories: 159 kcal, Protein: 6g, Fiber: 3g, Carbohydrates: 31g, Fat: 2g

107. Walnut and Raisin Bread

Prep Time: 10 minutes

Cook Time: 1 hour

Serves: 16 servings

Ingredients

3 cups of cool water

1 cup of walnuts, chopped

1 cup of raisins

2 tsp. salt

2 tsp. cinnamon, ground

2 tsp. active dry yeast

1/4 cup of sugar

6 cups of flour

Preparation

1. Add the salt, cinnamon, yeast, sugar, and flour to a big bowl and mix together.

2. Add water, raisins, and chopped walnuts to the flour mixture and mix until a dough is formed.

3. Cover the dough bowl and set aside for 7 to 8 hours at room temperature.

4. Place a lidded Dutch oven on the middle rack of an oven.

5. Heat up the oven to 450 degrees Fahrenheit for 30 minutes.

6. Transfer the dough to a floured work surface.

7. Shape the dough into a round shape and transfer it to the middle of a piece of parchment paper.

8. Score the dough with bread lame.

9. Transfer the dough to the hot Dutch oven with the parchment paper.

10. Cover the Dutch oven with the lid and bake the dough for 30 minutes.

11. Remove the Dutch oven lid and bake the bread until brown, or for 20 to 30 minutes.

Nutritional Information/Serving

Calories: 130 kcal, Protein: 3g, Fiber: 1g, Carbohydrates: 24g, Fat: 3g

108. Pumpkin Seed Bread

Prep Time: 10 minutes

Cook Time: 35 minutes

Serves: 10 servings

Ingredients

1 tablespoon of chia seeds

1 tablespoon of sunflower seeds

1 ½ tablespoons of pumpkin seeds

2 tablespoons of almond slices

1 teaspoon of salt

3 cups of bread flour

3 tablespoons of sugar

1 pack of rapid-rising yeast

1 ½ cups plus 2 tablespoons of water, warm

Preparation

1. Add all the seeds and bread flour to a big bowl and mix together.

2. Create a well in the middle of the flour mixture.

3. Add the remaining ingredients to a medium bowl and mix until combined.

4. Add the sugar mixture to the middle of the flour mixture and mix until a dough is formed.

5. On a floured work surface, transfer the dough and knead until a smooth texture is formed.

6. Shape the dough into a roughly ball shape and transfer to a greased bowl.

7. Use plastic wrap to cover the dough and set aside at room temperature for 1 hour, 30 minutes, or 2 hours.

8. Heat up an oven to 450 degrees Fahrenheit.

9. Return the dough to the floured work surface.

10. Press down the dough lightly, fold, and reshape into a round shape.

11. Transfer the shaped dough to a sheet of parchment paper with the seam side facing down.

12. Use bread lame to score the dough.

13. Place a lidded Dutch oven in the preheated oven for 15 to 20 minutes.

14. Transfer the dough to the Dutch oven with the parchment paper.

15. Cover the Dutch oven with a lid and bake the dough for 30 minutes.

16. Remove the Dutch oven lid and bake the bread until brown, or for 5 minutes.

17. Transfer the bread to a cooling rack to cool.

18. Serve or transfer the bread to a well-lidded container and store for 2 days at a warm temperature.

Nutritional Information/Serving

Calories: 193 kcal, Protein: 6.2g, Fiber: 2.3g, Carbohydrates: 35.4g, Fat: 2.9g

109. Quinoa Bread

Prep Time: 10 minutes

Cook Time: 45 minutes

Serves: 16 servings

Ingredients

4 cups of white flour

1½ teaspoons of salt

2 tablespoons of avocado oil

2 tablespoons of sugar, granulated

2¼ teaspoons of active dry yeast

½ cup of cooked quinoa

2 cups of water, lukewarm

Preparation

1. Add water and dry yeast to a big bowl and stir together.

2. Cover the yeast mixture and set it aside for 5 minutes.

3. Add the remaining ingredients to the yeast mixture and mix until a dough is formed.

4. Cover the dough bowl loosely and set aside for 1-2 hours at room temperature.

5. Shape the dough and transfer it to a lined Dutch oven.

6. Set aside the dough for 20–30 minutes.

7. Heat up an oven to 400 degrees Fahrenheit.

8. Transfer the Dutch oven to the preheated oven and bake the dough for 25–45 minutes.

Nutritional Information/Serving

Calories: 154 kcal, Protein: 4g, Fiber: 1g, Carbohydrates: 29g, Fat: 2g

110. Cashew Nut Bread

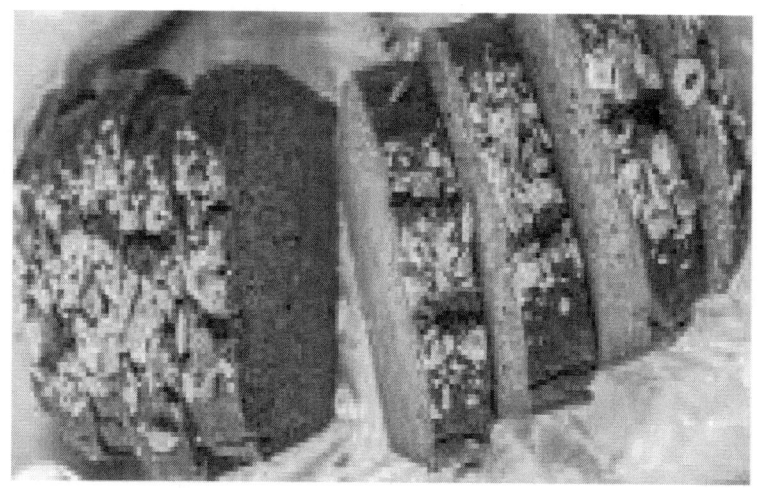

Prep Time: 10 minutes

Cook Time: 50 minutes

Serves: 12 servings

Ingredients

¼ cup of cashew nut pieces

¼ cup of dried blueberries

1 ⅝ cups of water

2 teaspoons of salt

½ teaspoon of active dry yeast

3 cups of white flour

Preparation

1. In a bowl, add the dry yeast, salt, and white flour and stir together.

2. Add the cashew nut and blueberries to the flour mixture and mix together.

3. Add the water to the flour mixture and mix until a dough is formed.

4. Use plastic wrap to tightly cover the dough bowl and set it aside for 12 hours at a warm temperature.

5. Place a lidded Dutch oven in an oven.

6. Heat up the oven to 450° Fahrenheit for 30 minutes.

7. Lightly sprinkle flour on the dough and shape it into a round shape.

8. Transfer the shaped dough to the middle of a piece of parchment paper.

9. Use plastic wrap to cover the dough and set aside for 30 minutes.

10. Use bread lame to score the top of the dough.

11. Transfer the dough with the parchment paper to the hot Dutch oven.

12. Cover the Dutch oven with a lid, and bake the dough for 35 minutes.

13. Remove the Dutch oven lid and bake the bread until brown, or for 10–15 minutes more.

Nutritional Information/Serving

Calories: 140 kcal, Protein: 3.7g, Fiber: 1g, Carbohydrates: 27.3g, Fat: 1.5g

111. Oat and Seed Bread

Prep Time: 10 minutes

Cook Time: 50 minutes

Serves: 10 servings

Ingredients

For Bread:

3 cups of water, warm

3 tsp. instant dry yeast

2 tsp. salt

2 tbsp. sesame seeds

1/3 cup of sunflower seeds

3 tbsp. flax seeds

2 tbsp. honey

1 1/2 cups of old-fashioned

6 cups of bread flour

For Topping:

2 tbsp. white seeds

1/4 cup of rolled oats

Preparation

1. Add dry yeast, salt, seeds, 1 1/2 cups of oats, and flour to a big bowl and mix together.

2. Add honey and warm water to the middle of the flour mixture, and mix until a dough is formed.

3. Use plastic wrap to cover the dough bowl and set it aside at room temperature for 60 minutes.

4. Gently punch down the dough and transfer it to the refrigerator for 8 hours.

5. Transfer the dough bowl to a counter for 3 hours.

6. Place a lidded Dutch oven in an oven.

7. Heat up the oven to 450° Fahrenheit for 30 minutes.

8. Transfer the dough to a lightly floured piece of parchment paper.

9. Tightly shape the dough into a round shape.

10. Use plastic wrap to cover the dough and set aside for 30 minutes.

11. Use bread lame to cut slits on the dough top.

12. Spray water on the top of the dough.

13. Sprinkle the white seeds and oats on the sides and top of the dough.

14. Transfer the dough with the parchment paper to the heated Dutch oven.

15. Use the lid to cover the Dutch and bake the dough for 30 minutes.

16. Remove the Dutch oven lid and bake the bread until brown, or for 20 minutes more.

Nutritional Information/Serving

Calories: 419 kcal, Protein: 14g, Fiber: 5g, Carbohydrates: 75g, Fat: 7g

112. Almond and Chia Seed Bread

Prep Time: 10 minutes

Cook Time: 45 minutes

Serves: 6 servings

Ingredients

1 1/2 cups of water

1/2 teaspoon east, active dry

1 tablespoon of chia seeds

1/8 cup slivered almonds

1/4 cup of cranberries, dried

3 cups of flour

Preparation

1. Add all the ingredients except water to a bowl and mix together.

2. Add water to the flour mixture and mix until combined.

3. Tightly cover the flour mixture with plastic wrap and set aside for 12 to 18 hours at a warm temperature.

4. Place a lidded Dutch oven in an oven.

5. Heat up the oven to 450° Fahrenheit for 30 minutes.

6. Sprinkle flour in the hot Dutch oven.

7. Shape the dough into a round shape.

8. Transfer the shaped dough to the hot Dutch oven and cover with the lid.

9. Bake the dough for 30 minutes.

10. Remove the Dutch oven lid and bake the bread until brown, or for 10 to 15 minutes more.

11. Transfer the bread to a cooling rack to cool, slice, and serve.

Nutritional Information/Serving

Calories: 316 kcal, Protein: 8.8g, Fiber: 3.8g, Carbohydrates: 55.8g, Fat: 6.4g

Chapter 11: Herbs and Spices Breads

113. Olive and Tomato Bread

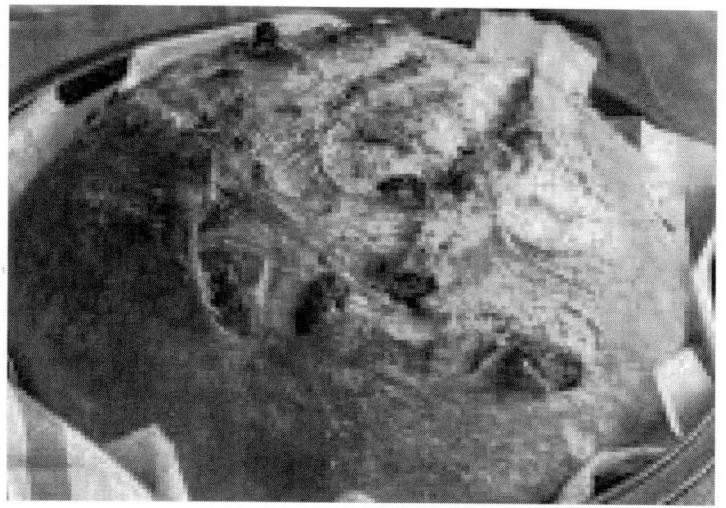

Prep Time: 10 minutes

Cook Time: 35 minutes

Serves: 8 servings

Ingredients

For Bread:

1 tbsp. of cornmeal (for dusting)

2 tbsp. of canola oil

4 cups of white flour

1/2 tsp. salt

1 cup of water, warm

1/2 tsp. sugar

2 tsp. active dry yeast

For Topping:

Parmesan cheese, grated

Basil, fresh

Italian Herbs

Pink salt

Sliced Campari tomatoes

Pitted black olives

Preparation

For Bread:

1. Add the salt and white flour to a big bowl and stir together.

2. In another bowl, add water, sugar, and yeast.

3. Set aside the yeast mixture for 2 minutes.

4. Pour the yeast mixture into the flour mixture and mix until a dough is formed.

5. Transfer the dough to a work surface and knead the dough for 10 minutes.

6. Drizzle the canola oil over the dough.

7. Use plastic wrap to cover the dough and set aside for 1-2 hours at room temperature.

8. Place a greased Dutch oven in an oven.

9. Heat up the oven to 425 degrees Fahrenheit for 2 minutes.

10. Sprinkle cornmeal in the warm Dutch oven.

11. Knead the dough again for a few minutes.

12. Transfer the dough to the Dutch oven and use a fork to poke the dough.

For Topping:

13. Lightly sprinkle the salt and Italian herbs over the top of the dough.

14. Add the olives and tomatoes on top of the dough and set aside for 3 to 4 minutes.

15. Place a lid on the Dutch oven and bake the dough for 20 minutes at 400 degrees Fahrenheit.

16. Remove the Dutch oven lid and bake the bread for an additional 10 to 15 minutes.

17. Set aside the bread for 10 minutes to cool.

18. Sprinkle the grated cheese over the bread.

19. Serve the bread with the basil.

Nutritional Information/Serving

Calories: 280 kcal, Protein: 7.2g, Fiber: 2g, Carbohydrates: 50.7g, Fat: 4.8g

114. Garlic and Tomato Bread

Prep Time: 10 minutes

Cook Time: 1 hour, 35 minutes

Serves: 8 servings

Ingredients

1 1/2 cups of water (at room temperature)

3 oz. tomatoes, sun-dried

1/2 tsp. yeast, active dry

1 3/4 tsp. of salt

3 cups of white flour (plus more for sprinkling)

1 tbsp. olive oil

1 head clove of garlic

Preparation

1. Heat up an oven to 425° Fahrenheit.

2. Use a knife to slice off the top of the garlic clove head.

3. Transfer the garlic to a big piece of aluminum foil.

4. Drizzle the oil over the garlic and wrap with foil.

5. For 45 minutes, roast the garlic head and transfer it to a plate to cool.

6. Chop the roasted garlic.

7. Add chopped garlic and the remaining ingredients and water to a big bowl and mix together.

8. Add water to the flour mixture and mix until a dough is formed.

9. Use plastic wrap to cover the dough and set aside for 12 to 18 hours at room temperature.

10. Place a lidded Dutch oven in the oven.

11. Heat up the oven to 450° Fahrenheit.

12. Use flour to dust a big sheet of parchment paper.

13. Shape the dough into a round shape and transfer it to the prepared parchment paper.

14. Transfer the dough with the parchment paper to the hot Dutch oven.

15. Cover the Dutch oven with a lid and bake the dough for 30 minutes.

16. Remove the Dutch oven lid and bake the bread until brown, or for 15 to 20 minutes more.

17. Transfer the bread to a cooling rack to cool, slice, and serve.

Nutritional Information/Serving

Calories: 190 kcal, Protein: 5.1g, Fiber: 1.5g, Carbohydrates: 36.6g, Fat: 2.2g

115. Herb-Rustic Bread

Prep Time: 10 minutes

Cook Time: 1 hour

Serves: 10 servings

Ingredients

Olive oil

3 cups of bread flour

2 tsp. coarse salt (plus extra for sprinkling)

1 tbsp. of freshly chopped herbs

1/2 cup of butter, unsalted

2 1/4 tsp. of active dry yeast

1 cup of water, warm

Preparation

1. In a bowl, add the dry yeast and water, stir together, and set aside for 5 minutes.

2. Place a small skillet over heat and add butter.

3. Take the skillet off the heat and add the chopped herbs to the hot butter.

4. Set aside the butter mixture to slightly cool.

5. Add coarse salt and 2 cups of flour to a mixing bowl and stir together.

6. Pour the yeast mixture into the flour mixture and mix together.

7. Add the butter mixture to the flour mixture and mix until a dough is formed.

8. Add the remaining bread flour to the dough and mix until combined.

9. Knead the dough for 5 minutes or until a smooth texture is formed.

10. Use plastic wrap to cover the dough and set aside for 60 minutes.

11. Heat an oven to 450° Fahrenheit.

12. Use parchment paper to line a Dutch oven.

13. Gently punch the dough down.

14. Knead the dough again for a couple of minutes and shape into a round shape.

15. Transfer the shaped dough to the lined Dutch oven.

16. Use bread lame to score the top of the dough.

17. Drizzle oil over the top of the dough.

18. Place a lid on the Dutch oven and set it aside for 10 minutes.

19. Transfer the Dutch oven to the preheated oven and bake the dough for 30 minutes.

20. Remove the Dutch oven lid and bake the bread until golden, or for 15 to 30 minutes.

21. Transfer the bread to a cooling rack to cool, slice, and serve.

Nutritional Information/Serving

Calories: 338 kcal, Protein: 10g, Fiber: 2g, Carbohydrates: 54g, Fat: 9g

116. No Knead Thyme Bread

Prep Time: 10 minutes

Cook Time: 45 minutes

Serves: 6 servings

Ingredients

1/4 cup of olive oil

1 1/4 cups of water (room temperature)

1 1/2 tablespoons of freshly chopped thyme

1 1/2 tablespoons of freshly chopped rosemary

1 1/2 teaspoons salt

1/2 teaspoon of instant yeast

3 cups of white flour

Preparation

1. Add the thyme, rosemary, salt, yeast, and white flour to a big bowl and mix together.

2. Add oil and water to the flour mixture and mix until a dough is formed.

3. Use plastic wrap to cover the dough bowl and set aside for 10 to 18 hours at room temperature.

4. Transfer the dough to a floured work surface, fold, and shape the dough into a round shape.

5. Transfer the dough to a lightly greased piece of parchment paper.

6. Use a damp tea towel to cover the dough and set aside for 1 to 1 hour, 30 minutes.

7. Place a lidded Dutch oven in an oven.

8. Heat up the oven to 500° Fahrenheit for 30 minutes.

9. Use bread lame to score the top of the dough.

10. Transfer the dough with the parchment paper to the hot Dutch oven and cover with a lid.

11. Reduce the oven heat to 425° Fahrenheit and bake the dough for 30 minutes.

12. Remove the Dutch oven lid and bake the bread for 15 minutes more.

13. Transfer the bread to a cooling rack to cool, slice, and serve.

Nutritional Information/Serving

Calories: 309 kcal, Protein: 6.6g, Fiber: 1.9g, Carbohydrates: 48.1g, Fat: 9.7g

117. Parmesan Rosemary Bread

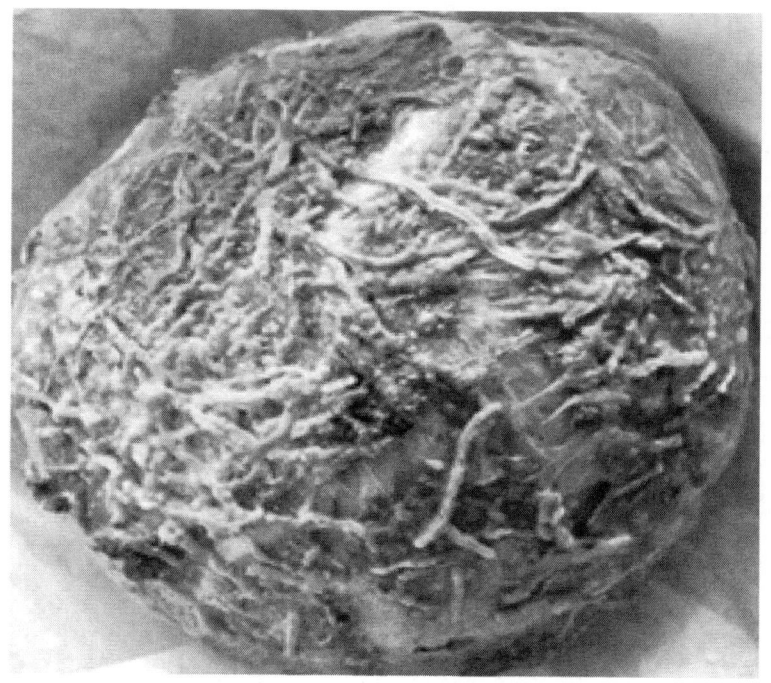

Prep Time: 10 minutes

Cook Time: 45 minutes

Serves: 6 servings

Ingredients

312 g of cool water

1 tbsp. freshly minced rosemary

15 g of grated parmesan cheese

2 g of instant yeast

7 g of kosher salt

390 g of flour

Preparation

1. In a big mixing bowl, add all the ingredients except water and mix together.

2. Slowly add the water to the flour mixture and mix until a dough is formed.

3. Use plastic wrap to cover the dough bowl and set aside for 18 to 20 minutes.

4. Place a lidded Dutch oven in an oven.

5. Heat up the oven to 450 degrees Fahrenheit for 40 minutes.

6. Sprinkle flour on a work surface and transfer the dough to the surface.

7. Lightly dust the top of the dough with flour.

8. Loosely shape the dough into a square shape.

9. Roll up the dough into a log shape.

10. Transfer the shaped dough to the middle of a piece of parchment paper.

11. Use a tea towel to cover the dough and set it aside for 20 minutes.

12. Use bread lame to score the top of the dough.

13. Transfer the dough with the parchment paper to the hot Dutch oven.

14. Cover the Dutch oven with a lid, and bake the dough for 30 minutes.

15. Remove the Dutch oven lid and bake the bread until brown, or for 10 to 15 minutes.

16. Transfer the bread to a wire rack to cool, slice, and serve.

Nutritional Information/Serving

Calories: 266 kcal, Protein: 7.9g, Fiber: 1.9g, Carbohydrates: 54.2g, Fat: 1.4g

118. Rosemary-Yeast Bread

Prep Time: 10 minutes

Cook Time: 50 minutes

Serves: 8 servings

Ingredients

1½ cups of water (at room temperature)

½ tsp. of active dry yeast

¾ cup of freshly chopped rosemary leaves

1¾ tsp. salt

3 cups of flour

Preparation

1. Add all the ingredients except water to a big bowl and stir together.

2. Add the water to the flour mixture and mix until it combines.

3. Use plastic wrap to cover the flour mixture bowl and set aside for 8 to 12 hours at a warm temperature.

4. Place a lidded Dutch oven in an oven.

5. Heat up the oven to 450 degrees Fahrenheit.

6. Sprinkle flour on a work surface and transfer the dough to the surface.

7. Fold and shape the dough into a round shape.

8. Transfer the dough to the hot Dutch oven and cover with a lid.

9. Bake the dough for 30 minutes.

10. Remove the Dutch oven lid and bake the bread until brown, or for 15 to 20 minutes more.

11. Transfer the bread to a cooling rack to cool.

12. Serve the bread or transfer it to a well-lidded container and store for 3 days or freeze for 3 months.

Nutritional Information/Serving

Calories: 176 kcal, Protein: 5g, Fiber: 2g, Carbohydrates: 37g, Fat: 1g

119. Garlic Bread

Prep Time: 10 minutes

Cook Time: 40 minutes

Serves: 16 servings

Ingredients

5 (smashed) garlic cloves

2 tbsp. of Italian seasoning

1 ½ cups of water, lukewarm

1/2 tsp. of yeast

2 tsp. of salt

3 cups of white flour

Preparation

1. Add the yeast, salt, and white flour to a big bowl and stir together.

2. Add the lukewarm water to the flour mixture and mix until a dough is formed.

3. Use oil-sprayed plastic wrap to cover the dough bowl and set aside for 12 to 18 hours.

4. Place a lidded Dutch oven in an oven.

5. Heat up the oven to 450 degrees Fahrenheit for 30 minutes.

6. Transfer the dough to a well-floured surface and shape into a round shape.

7. Cover the dough and set it aside for 30 minutes.

8. Transfer the dough to the hot Dutch oven.

9. Sprinkle the smashed garlic and the Italian seasoning over the dough.

10. Cover the Dutch oven with a lid, and bake the dough for 30 minutes.

11. Remove the Dutch oven lid and bake the bread for 10 minutes more.

12. Transfer the bread to a wire rack to cool, slice, and serve.

Nutritional Information/Serving

Calories: 89 kcal, Protein: 2g, Fiber: 1g, Carbohydrates: 18g, Sodium: 292mg

120. Dill and Cheese Bread

Prep Time: 10 minutes

Cook Time: 30 minutes

Serves: 8 servings

Ingredients

1 tablespoon of dill, dried

1 1/4 cup of cheddar cheese, shredded

1 teaspoon of salt

4 cups of white flour

1 pack of dry yeast

1 tablespoon of sugar

1 1/2 cups of warm water

Preparation

1. In a bowl, add the sugar and warm water and mix until it dissolves.

2. Add the dry yeast to the sugar mixture and stir together.

3. Set aside the sugar mixture for 5 to 10 minutes.

4. Add 3 cups of the white flour and salt to another bowl and mix together.

5. Slowly add the sugar mixture to the flour mixture and mix until a dough is formed.

6. Add the dill, a cup of the shredded cheese, and the remaining flour to the dough bowl.

7. Mix on low speed until it combines.

8. Shape the dough into a round shape.

9. Use plastic wrap to cover the dough and set aside for 60 minutes at room temperature.

10. Use a piece of parchment paper to line a Dutch oven.

11. Heat up an oven to 450° Fahrenheit.

12. Gently punch down the dough and reshape it into a round shape.

13. Transfer the shaped dough to the lined Dutch oven.

14. Sprinkle the remaining cheese on the top of the dough.

15. Bake the dough in the preheated oven until golden, or for 30 minutes.

Nutritional Information/Serving

Calories: 264 kcal, Protein: 8.2g, Fiber: 1.7g, Carbohydrates: 49.4g, Fat: 3.2g

END

Thank you for reading my book.

Carlena B. Reese

Printed in Great Britain
by Amazon

54792010R00212